*Comfort for the
Losses in Life*

Comfort for the Losses in Life

How the God of All Comfort Will Meet You in Your

Grief

Doubt

Disappointment

Confusion

Loneliness

DAVID E. ROSAGE

CHARIS

Servant Publications
Ann Arbor, Michigan

All Scripture quotations are from the New American Bible for Catholics, © 1970 by the Confraternity of Christian Doctrine, Washington, D.C., including the Revised New Testament, © 1986. All rights reserved.

Charis Books is an imprint of Servant Publications especially designed to serve Roman Catholics.

Published by Servant Publications
P.O. Box 8617
Ann Arbor, Michigan 48107

Cover design by Janice Hendrick, Good Visuals

95 96 97 98 99 10 9 8 7 6 5 4 3 2 1

Printed in the United States of America
ISBN 0-89283-887-6

Library of Congress Cataloging-in-Publication Data

Rosage, David E.
    Comfort for the losses in life : how the God of all comfort will meet you in your grief, doubt, disappointment, confusion, loneliness / David E. Rosage.
        p.   cm.
    Includes bibliographical references.
    ISBN 0-89283-887-6
    1. Consolation.   2. Peace of mind—Religious aspects—Catholic Church.   3. Christian life—Catholic authors.   4. Loss (Psychology)—Religious aspects—Christianity.   5. Adjustment (Psychology)—Religous aspects—Christianity.   I. Title.
BX2350.2.R655   1995
248.8'6—dc20   95-823
                                                                          CIP

Contents

SECTION II: FINDING GOD IN THE SEASONS AND CIRCUMSTANCES OF LIFE

Acknowledgments

I am deeply grateful to

the many wounded people who
shared their heartaches with me,

Armand Nigro, SJ, for his theological guidance,

Marvin Lavoy for his psychological suggestions,

Thelma Pohl for her valuable critique and insights,

Maxine Keogh for the many hours spent in editing
and preparing the manuscript.

Introduction

For a number of years, I have been privileged to be a companion for many wonderful people who were suffering various kinds of losses—be it a loss of their own good health, the death of a loved one, loss of employment, a breakup of a marriage, or one of the many other kinds of painful losses. I walked with them, listened to them, empathized with them, comforted them, encouraged them, prayed with them. In nearly all cases they taught me very much and enabled me to accept the little crosses that occasionally creep into my life. My admiration and appreciation of these people enduring grave losses increased every time I met them.

In this volume I have captured the struggles of many of these men and women, describing the challenges common to all of them in a way that protects the identities of each individual. These accounts are offered herein for a twofold purpose: to encourage anyone enduring a heavy loss; secondly, to be a resource for those who are personally concerned with someone experiencing a serious loss. For this reason *Comfort for the Losses in Life* is divided into two sections.

SECTION I

In the first section, chapters one to five outline the necessary attitudes and dispositions required for accepting, enduring, and eventually recovering from a grave loss. Our ability to recover will depend largely on a fourfold relationship we must develop: our relationship with God, with ourselves, with others, and

11

with the Lord's creation. As we strive to develop these four channels of relationships, we will not only be able to survive our pain, but eventually enjoy the peace of mind and heart that every human being craves.

SECTION II

Chapters six to sixteen delve into specific situations that people experience in life that threaten to rob them of the God-given gift of peace they desire. In each case the afflicted are encouraged to maintain and deepen their contact with God. This is done by keeping themselves aware of his boundless love for them and by asking for his grace and assistance to survive any loss he may permit to come their way. When they ask for the enlightenment to recognize his will in their afflictions, they will eventually experience the love, life, and peace the Lord intends for them.

God permits tragedy to visit us because of its inherent potential to mature and mold us into better people. We mention only one of the countless people who have been transformed through suffering. Rembrandt was one of the world's greatest artists. After his wife died, he suffered from depression and painted very poorly. After some time he reached the stage of acceptance and bounced back to paint with a new vigor and purpose. Today the world enjoys the fruit of his painful transformation as it is revealed in his art.

Ordinarily, the Lord does not heal us immediately. In the various accounts related herein, notice how those suffering losses sometimes had to be led through several stages of their personal feelings and reactions: from disbelief through anger, bargaining, and depression, until finally they were able to say yes to the Lord.

It is our hope and prayer that *Comfort for the Losses in Life* will also be helpful for those persons—angels of mercy—who care for the afflicted or minister to them in any way. Hopefully, it will help them understand the moods and temperaments of those in pain. It would be gratifying to know that those persons who are trying to help others survive their losses would find insights in these pages, enabling them to be patient and understanding with the afflicted who may be locked in one or more of the five stages of grief.

If we ourselves are suffering a grave loss, or if we are accompanying someone who is experiencing a heavy burden or loss, may our prayer always be:

"Blessed be the God and Father of our Lord Jesus Christ, the Father of compassion and God of all encouragement, who encourages us in our every affliction, so that we may be able to encourage those who are in any affliction with the encouragement with which we ourselves are encouraged by God."   **2 Corinthians 1:3-4**

SECTION I

*How to
Find True Peace*

ONE

—▶●◀—

Why, Lord?

Some time ago the Twenty Questions game was a popular pastime. One player would select a person without revealing his or her identity to the rest of the players. In turn the others would ask questions, hoping to identify the selected person. The questions were posed in such a way that the first player would reply only with a no or yes—no other details would be given.

When suffering and pain come into our lives, we often try to play the question game with God. We bombard him with questions hoping to find some answer to the mystery of suffering. Why, Lord? Why me? Why at this time? What have I done to deserve this pain? Why so many tragic and traumatic happenings in life? We are like the little lad tagging after his father with an endless series of "Why, Daddy?"

The greatest minds have asked the same questions, but the answer still remains elusive and will continue to defy definition. Even though we cannot fully understand the purpose of suffering, we have experienced many of its fruits. We know from personal experience that when all is going well in life, we think of the Lord less often than when problems and pain arise.

Pain is a purifying process enabling us to rise above mundane concerns that occupy so much of our time, energy, and attention, to focus on those things that really matter in life. When we are confronted with grave suffering and the possibility of death, our attitude changes toward the former projects and programs in which we were involved. Life's prospects seem to be continually altered for our own welfare.

I remember my mother kneading bread. She would punch it down, only to have it rise again on its way to becoming some of the best bread I ever tasted. Through pain, suffering and disappointment, the Lord kneads us into becoming much better people. The Chinese word for "crisis" comes from the symbols for two other words—the symbol for "danger" and the symbol for "opportunity." Every crisis is a new opportunity for us to grow and develop into a stronger more mature person.

When suffering seems to overwhelm us, we often ask the question, "Why, Lord?" The question we should ask ourselves is this: How is God present for us in suffering and how can we find peace in our pain? The surest path to peace is the realization that the Lord is with us at every moment of the day and that he will bring good out of everything that comes our way. Suffering is a test of our faith and enables it to grow stronger and deeper with every experience of pain.

Jesus, our teacher par excellence, used parables and metaphors to explain obscure truths and give us some understanding of his way of life. In the parable of the vine and the branches, he gives us a better understanding of suffering. He tells us that we will be pruned not simply to bear fruit, but to bear even more fruit. Suffering and pruning are painful, but they enable us to bear much fruit.

Jesus also referred to his own death and to our dying to self, "Amen, amen, I say to you, unless a grain of wheat falls to the ground and dies, it remains just a grain of wheat, but if it dies, it produces much fruit. Whoever loves his life loses it, and whoever hates his life in this world will preserve it for eternal life" (Jn 12:24f).

Suffering and pain enable us to die to self-centered concerns and to elevate our focus to the Lord.

In his autobiography, *Journal Of A Soul*, Pope John XXIII passed on to us many guidelines for our own journey through life. Concerning suffering he wrote:

Above all, one must always be ready for the Lord's surprise moves, for though he treats his loved ones well, he generally likes to test them with all sorts of trials, such as bodily infirmities, bitterness of soul, and sometimes opposition so powerful as to transform and wear out the life of the servant of servants of God, making it a real martyrdom....[1]

Trials and tribulations help to form who we are. No one has been strengthened and transformed into a gracious, kind person by living an easy life.

The testing and trials that Pope John XXIII mentions include physical, emotional, and spiritual sufferings. Recalling people afflicted in any way may help us recognize our own hardships and lead us into a healing process.

DOUBLE WHAMMY

Jim showed me a letter from his wife, the mother of their four children; he found the letter on his desk when he arrived home from work. She informed him that she was tired of being tied down seven days a week caring for him, the children and their large home. She was leaving with a boyfriend to begin life anew, free from the drudgery of slaving for them. She never wanted to see him again nor the children who were such a burden to her.

Jim was stunned and heartbroken. He could not believe the content of the letter—he had never suspected that she was seeing someone else. Although he was aware that the family sapped much of her strength, he never realized that she was so miserable. Grief-stricken, he asked many times, "Why, Lord? What did I do wrong? Where do we go from here?" As the weeks dragged on, Jim's sadness was deepened by the fact that the children missed their mother and asked countless questions about her. Some of the children had guilt feelings wondering if they were the cause of her leaving.

The only advice I could give him was to have faith and trust in the Lord and try to get on with life for the sake of the children. With the help of hired housekeepers, Jim coped with the situation to the best of his ability, but his eyes were saddened, his cheerful smile was gone, and his whole disposition changed radically.

Some years later as Jim was still trying to adjust to his loss, another tragedy loomed up in his life. His eldest son John, a detective on the city police force, was fatally shot by a gang member. Jim's world came apart once again. As he agonized over the brutal death of his son, he became angry and was tormented day and night with thoughts of hatred and revenge.

After the murderer was apprehended and the date set for the trial some months later, the district attorney sent Jim a letter asking for some facts about John's life and personality. The last question enkindled anew his anger and bitterness. "What sentence would you recommend for the man who shot your son?" Jim clenched his fist and pounded his desk, his mind and heart filled with thoughts of hatred and revenge. He struggled with the last question for days without being able to find the answer. Weary and exhausted, he sat down one evening in his living room, still wrestling with these horrible thoughts. His gaze caught sight of a picture of John on the mantle over the fireplace. Above it hung a large crucifix. As he stared at the crucifix for nearly an hour, the plaintive words of Jesus echoed in his heart, "Father, forgive them, they know not what they do" (Lk 23:34). His tear-filled eyes returned to the picture of John, smiling down on him, while tormenting thoughts raced through his mind. He jumped up, went over to his desk and clenching his pen he responded to the last question on the DA's letter, "Please... tell that man I forgive him." As he sat back in his chair, a calm came over him—and a healing was freeing him from his anger. Wounded and scarred, Jim resolved to get on with his life with the Lord's help.

Jim was able to survive this agonizing ordeal because his faith convinced him that in some mysterious way this fit into God's plans.

When suffering, pain, tragedy, and injustice come our way, we ought to acknowledge our angry feelings before they go underground and cause depression within us. Depression is a terrible affliction, devastating our whole personality. We can be immobilized, uninterested and unable to communicate or make decisions. Depression can make us unbearably lonely and frustrated with friends and family. Jim avoided depression by recognizing that his feelings of anger and disbelief were a process of coping with tragedy. He survived it all by his faith in God.

TYPES OF SUFFERING

As integrated persons we are created with a physical, emotional, and spiritual nature; pain and suffering are classified under these same three aspects. However valid such a distinction may be, any kind of suffering takes its toll on our whole being. All suffering is interrelated, even though some ailments may be listed as physical, emotional, or spiritual. A severe headache may be physical, but it affects our whole person, causing us to be more easily impatient with others, or more listless and less interested in favorite projects that require concentration. Tension, worry, anxiety, or the loss of a close friendship may be listed as emotional pain, but they also disrupt our physical well-being. We suffer spiritually when we are plagued with scruples, a sense of guilt or remorse. We may also be distressed by the distractions or dryness we experience in prayer.

Our whole personality reflects this interior turmoil. It is evident that any form of suffering influences our whole personality.

Physical Infirmities. When Ralph was grounded with an attack of influenza, he was exasperated because he had to cancel important meetings. With the urging and prayers of his wife, he was gradually reconciled to his illness and began to relax.

Agnes, a single parent with three children, was plagued with severe back pains over a long period of time. When the pain became intolerable, she was informed that the only remedy was orthopedic surgery followed by considerable time for recuperation. She was greatly distraught. How could she keep up her household and care for her children? Her anxiety intensified her suffering. When her mother, who lived in a distant city, called to assure her that she was coming to care for her and the children and would stay as long as needed, Agnes was greatly relieved and found some peace of mind as she agreed to the surgery.

Mike complained constantly because of the restrictions and limitations the passing years inflicted upon him. He regretted that he could not do all the things he was accustomed to doing. With the passing of time, he became resigned to his condition and found new projects to undertake in his old age.

Martha's terminal illness brought a cloud of gloom over her family. Her own quiet acceptance of God's will enabled her to radiate peace and joy to all her loved ones.

We can be certain that for these sufferers, there were moments of disbelief, some anger, perhaps some bargaining with God, and eventually acceptance and peace.

Emotional Suffering. Marie was so jealous of her husband's attention that she mistrusted him for no reason. She refused to attend social gatherings lest some woman be attracted to him. She lost most of her friends because of her attitude and made life miserable for her husband.

Robert, a junior in high school, was crushed—his world was

shattered. He had fallen in love with Judy some weeks before, only to have her shower her attention on another student.

Elmer, a veteran of World War II, suffered serious shrapnel wounds in his arm and legs. He was advised to apply for total disability and to exercise his legs daily to retain the use of them. He became depressed, fearing that he would be handicapped for life, but in the midst of his depression an inspiration came to him. He applied and was accepted as a mail carrier, which gave him a new lease on life and plenty of exercise.

He enjoyed many cheerful encounters on his mail route. One such instance was an elderly woman who could no longer see to read. Each time she received a first-class letter, Elmer put down his bag and read it to her, such was his gentle disposition. Gradually, his depression disappeared and his happy, cheerful disposition radiated to everyone he met.

At his funeral the large parish church was filled to capacity. Many of those who came to pray and pay their last respects were his friends on his mail route. With the Lord's help, Elmer was able to break the tentacles of depression, to enrich his own life and the lives of many others. He was at peace.

Another emotional problem that afflicts people is worry or anxiety. Of people who worry unduly, Anna would come close to the top of the list. She worries about happenings locally as well as worldwide. She worries constantly about her happily married children, wondering if someday a divorce will creep into their lives. She is anxiety-ridden about her grandchildren growing up in our mixed-up world. She even worries when all is going well since she has nothing to worry about. Fortunately, she recognizes her propensity to worry and is struggling to overcome it. Her parish priest advised her to pray daily the words of the Our Father at Mass, "Deliver us, Lord, from every evil... and protect us from all anxiety...." With these words of faith, she would be rescued by power of prayer.

Spiritual Suffering. Having suffered a stroke, Sheila was disappointed that she could no longer pray as she formerly did.

She regrets that all she can do now when she thinks about the Lord is to give a big sigh of awe and wonder at his goodness to her. When she was assured that a sigh could be the most perfect prayer she could offer in her condition, a broad smile reflected her relief.

Every time Rita thought about the woman who lured her husband away from her and the family, her anger blazed up anew. Her dreams of a home and loving family were gone. Anger, resentment, and revenge crowded her mind and heart many times throughout the day. Rita was well aware of the Lord's teaching about the necessity of forgiving others in order to be forgiven (Mt 6:14f). How could she ever forgive this woman? She had asked the Lord to remove the hatred from her heart, but she seemed unable to make any progress in generating feelings of forgiveness. Her anxiety over this lack of forgiveness added to her pain.

When someone explained to her that there is a difference between forgiving and forgetting, and that it is more difficult to forget than to forgive, she found a ray of hope in her struggle.

Forgiveness is a choice—a decision, not a feeling. Furthermore, in order to forgive we need the Lord's help as we pray, "Forgive us our trespasses as we forgive those who trespass against us." The Lord looks at our intentions—do we want to forgive? Are we taking any positive steps to try to forgive? Even though Rita's heart is heavy, her anxiety over a lack of forgiveness seems to be diminishing as she continues to ask for the grace to forgive.

Scrupulosity is a terrible affliction. Dick is inclined to be scrupulous and he worries constantly about his past sins. He knows that the Lord is a merciful, forgiving God, but he is troubled about the Lord's forgiveness touching him. Was he sufficiently sorry for his sins? Did he take proper measures to get over them? These and dozens of other anxieties trouble him. Only in the quiet prayer of listening to the Lord's Word reminding us of his love, mercy, and compassion will Dick be convinced of the Lord's eagerness to forgive more than we could want it ourselves.

PERSONAL AND COMMUNITY SURVIVAL

Nestled in the heart of the Rocky Mountains is Butte, Montana, with its "richest hill on earth." This former mining town is the place that Bob and Joyce O'Bill call home. When they learned that Joyce had to undergo serious emergency surgery they were shocked. They prayed fervently for a successful surgery and a complete recovery. To implement his prayer, Bob promised to build in his backyard a three- or four-foot statue in honor of Our Lady if Joyce was restored to good health.

During the anxious days of Joyce's illness, her friends and neighbors were deeply concerned about her survival. Fortunately, Joyce not only survived but regained good health. Faithful to his promise, Bob began laying plans for erecting the statue of Our Lady to express his gratitude to the Lord and Our Lady for his wife's recovery. As Bob shared his plans for building a little grotto, the whole idea burgeoned into a mammoth challenge for the whole community.

In order to appreciate the magnitude of what was beginning, we need to take a look at the prevailing conditions in the city of Butte. For generations, billions of dollars worth of copper, silver, and gold were mined from this "richest hill on earth." The people of Butte were accustomed to the hard work of mining and the economy had been good. However, with the fall in prices, the mines were closed and the hearts of the people sank deeper than their deepest mining pit. Unemployment rose, the economy was shattered, and a pall of hopelessness shrouded the city. People were depressed; many moved away while others waited anxiously for an uncertain future.

Bob O'Bill's dream of a backyard grotto became a challenging community project. Members of the whole community set aside their individual religious convictions, and with unwavering enthusiasm and determination began to plan a ninety-foot steel statue of Our Lady on the top of the continental divide. Committees were formed, men who were out of work volunteered their skills and services, materials were gathered, funds were raised, and soon they began to build a structure that took five years to complete.

The results were astounding. The 51-ton "Lady" was built and its four sections lifted 3,500 feet above Butte to the continental divide by Sikorsky Sky Crane of the Nevada Air National Guard team. The project was completed on December 20, 1985.

Our Lady of the Rockies has become a national and international shrine attracting thousands of tourists each year, which has helped the depleted economy of this once prosperous community. More important, it has welded a strong community spirit among them and brought hope and encouragement to a once depressed city. It has spelled economic survival for the people of Butte.

PEACE EVEN IN PAIN

In the midst of the pain and suffering, the misfortunes and heartaches of life, we often hear the refrain of "Why, Lord? Why me, Lord? Why at this time, Lord?" The Lord does not respond to our questioning by revealing the mystery of suffering, nor does he offer any reasons, but he makes pain more tolerable by leading us down the pathway of acceptance toward the blessings of peace of heart and mind. Did not Jesus promise, "Peace I leave with you; my peace I give you.... Do not let your hearts be troubled or afraid" (Jn 14:27).

Enlightened by the Spirit, we will gradually discover that genuine interior peace will depend on our fourfold relationship. When we are convinced that God is our Father who loves us unconditionally, we will find peace; when we are able to accept ourselves as we are with all our gifts and shortcomings, peace will reign in our hearts; when we recognize others as our brothers and sisters in the family of God, we will have reached the third level of peace. Finally, when we enjoy all the blessings of creation as well as the limitations our created human nature may impose on us, we will enjoy the fourth level of peace.

In the following chapters, we will reflect further on these different levels of peace.

Prayer

Lord Jesus, I know that you will never permit anything to happen to me which is not for my own good; yet, in my humanness, I cringe and complain when suffering and sorrow, trials and tribulations come into my life. Be with me always, as you promised, to strengthen and sustain me to accept willingly my daily cross and follow in your footsteps. Amen

TWO

At Peace with God, Our Father

On my first visit to the old city of Jerusalem, I was pleasantly surprised to hear on the crowded streets and in the busy bazaars the constant greeting *"shalom."* It is the customary greeting in Israel, inadequately translated in our language as "peace." Shalom may have fared much like our farewell greeting goodbye, often contracted into a simple "'bye." Goodbye comes to us so naturally that we may not always appreciate its significance. It is really a prayer and a blessing. Goodbye is a contraction of "God be with you"—to protect and guide you, to comfort and strengthen you, to love you and fill you with his peace.

The Hebrew word *shalom* is also a prayerful wish. It is a sort of umbrella word embracing the sum total of all the spiritual and material blessings here in this life, culminating in the gift of salvation and eternal peace. Peace means different things for different people. Some think of peace as a time when there are no military hostilities raging. For others, it is a time of quiet

29

and tranquility when problems, worries, and anxieties are fewer than usual.

For a mother of young children, it may mean a time when the children are snug in their beds and quiet reigns throughout the house. A cartoon portrayed a little girl tugging at her mother's apron asking: "Mom, why did you say that you would go crazy if I asked one more question?"

DISCOVERY

Harold was a successful businessman, respected and feared in the business community. He prided himself on the fact that he was a self-made man and did not rely on anyone else, not even on God. In fact, he was disappointed and often angry with God who seemed to let him down time after time. When Harold asked God for help in certain business ventures, for example, they always seemed to fail.

In his busy life, Harold had little time for God since he frequently had to travel on weekends or he chose to get some exercise and relaxation, which he found on the golf course rather than in church. Harold spent little time with his family and they were obviously growing farther apart; his friends were few. In spite of all his material success, Harold was a miserable, unhappy person. He was restless and lonely. Nothing seemed to satisfy him. He was always striving for more lucrative deals. He was proud of his business acumen, but he knew no peace, that precious gift from the Lord.

A sudden illness hospitalized Harold for several weeks, followed by a longer period of recuperation. This gave him time to reflect on the lack of warmth from his wife and family. His friends seldom, if ever, called. His business associates were disinterested. He longed for the serenity of mind and heart others seemed to enjoy. Finally, in desperation he cried out to God for help in finding peace and joy in his life.

There are many "Harolds" in our society. Perhaps we may at

times be numbered among them. Unwittingly we become so engrossed in the busyness of life, in various programs and projects, that we lose our focus on the important things that could bring us peace and fulfillment. In pursuit of many of these goals, we become exhausted and frustrated without satisfying our human desire for recognition and acceptance. Unfulfilled, we may end up in disappointment and even depression.

AT PEACE WITH GOD

The first major step toward attaining genuine peace of mind and heart in all the ups and downs in life is to examine our relationship with the Lord. Peace is the fruit of good personal relationships on four different levels: peace with the Lord, with ourselves, with our neighbor, and with creation. If we are to surmount and survive all the sufferings and sorrows, all the misfortunes and tragedies of life, we must be at peace on these four levels. Here we will reflect on the first level, peace with God.

Our life may need some re-focusing if we are to satisfy the longing of our heart for fulfillment and peace. Peace, first of all, is the fruit of our personal relationship with God, our loving Father. We deepen and enrich our relationship with the Lord by keeping ourselves ever aware of his unconditional, unchanging love for us, regardless of who we are or what we have done. He shares his creative, providential, forgiving love freely, so that we may pass that love on to others.

There are some faulty notions about the God of the Old Testament. Some question his love and kindness and regard him as a vengeful God, eager to punish any infraction of the law he promulgated. Contrary to these erroneous opinions, the God of the Old Testament is a loving, provident God and the only source of genuine peace. He is called "Yahweh Shalom," God of Peace (Jgs 6:24). He made a covenant of peace with his people and promised that it would never be shaken, come what may (Is 54:10). He promised them the Messiah who would be identified as the Prince of Peace (Is 9:5). By his redemptive death, the Prince of Peace restored our severed relations with the Father and endowed us with that peace, which the world cannot give. The many dimensions of his divine love touch every area of life.

LOVE CREATES

God's creative love fashioned our body as the most perfect machine ever devised. He created us a little less than the angels (Ps 8:6). Moses asks us, "Is he not your father who created you? Has he not made you and established you" (Dt 32:6ff). With the gift of sight we can see an object on the distant horizon or read a printed page close at hand. Our God-given gift of hearing enables us to enjoy good music, the laughter of children, the words of affection whispered in our ear. The dexterity of our hands makes it possible for us to pick up a tiny pin, move a heavy object, type a flawless page, or play the piano. Our sense of touch brings us pleasure as we cuddle a tiny infant, receive a healing hug, or feel the warmth of a friendly handshake.

GOD'S PROVIDENTIAL LOVE

The Lord's providential love is dynamic and operative at every moment in our lives, for he holds us in the palm of his hand (Is 49:16). The oxygen we inhale over 25,000 times each day manifests his providing love. The odyssey of a potato, from its planting to being served on the dinner table, is another proof of his concerned love. Jesus assures us that the Father who cares for the birds of the sky knows all our needs and all these things will be given us (Mt 6:26ff). The love of family and friends is another dimension of the Lord's providential, caring, and concerned love for us.

GOD'S FORGIVING LOVE

Peace fills our heart and soul knowing that the Lord's loving mercy, compassion, and forgiveness cleanse us when our own willfulness leads us into sin. He is always reaching out to grasp us by the hand when we have deviated from the way of life he mapped out for us. How comforting are the Father's words, "Fear not, for I have redeemed you; I have called you by name; you are mine" (Is 43:1). Even though our sinfulness may cause us some anxiety, the Lord is always eager to forgive for he says, "My love shall never leave you nor my covenant of peace be shaken" (Is 54:10). Jesus assured all those who came to him that their sins were forgiven. If we let him, Jesus will continue his redemptive pardoning and healing in our lives. Pardon brings that peace which the world cannot give.

RESPONDING TO GOD'S LOVE
IN GOOD TIMES AND BAD

Knowing with our heart that the Lord loves us unconditionally fills us with euphoria and genuine peace. That peace can be greatly increased as we strive to respond to his love. Love always awaits a loving response, otherwise it is a rejected love. When we love someone, we try to please that person. Likewise, divine love awaits our loving response. Prayerful reflection on the Lord's magnanimous love will instill a desire to do everything to please our gracious God. There is no selfish concern in God's love. The more generous our response, the more pleasing it is to our Father; our loving him makes us peaceful, happy people.

As a response to the Lord's infinite love, God desires that we live in conformity with his divine will in all the events of our daily routine. We are loving him when we strive to discern his will in the happenings of the day and to live in tune with his will. Experiencing his love will enable us to discern his will in problems and pains, in trials and tribulations, in joys and sorrows. We encounter nothing in life which is not either his direct will or his permissive will for our good. When our burdens are heavy and our duties seem unpleasant, we should remember that the Lord is with us carrying most of the load.

PEACEFUL OBEDIENCE

As we constantly strive to be aware of the Father's boundless love for us, we will be more inclined to accept and willingly fulfill whatever the Lord permits to come into our life. He will enable us to understand that nothing can happen to us from which he cannot bring some good for our spiritual growth. With his enlightenment we will then realize that doing whatever he asks of us is our way of responding in love to the outpouring of his love. This conviction enriches our relationship with the Lord which is the source of genuine peace.

The other three levels of peace—peace with ourselves, with others, and with creation—flow from this first level. In the next chapters we will reflect on achieving genuine peace in these other areas.

Prayer

Yahweh Shalom, Father of peace, bless us with your peace.
Jesus, Prince of Peace, grant us your peace.
Holy Spirit, Source of Peace, fill us with your peace.
Mary, Queen of Peace, pray that we may enjoy genuine peace.
                                                          Amen

THREE

At Peace with Ourselves

Tom was a gifted young man, but he was restless, bored with life, often discouraged and depressed. He was searching for something to satisfy the void in his life. After he inherited some money from his parents' estate, he decided to do some traveling with the hope of finding that missing piece in his life. On weekends and holidays he traveled to different states and into Canada, always searching, seeking.

During a brief sojourn in a metropolitan city, he was weary, lonely, homesick, desperate. After the untimely death of his parents he felt very much alone, having no one with whom he could share his feelings. While pacing the streets he stopped in front of a large stone church and was drawn to enter its huge doors. He sat quietly in the semidarkness for a long time before his attention rested on a large banner depicting Our Lady with the caption in large gold letters "Mary, Queen of Peace." He remembered that his own mother always seemed to be at peace, regardless of what the day might bring. He began to realize that peace was lacking in his life. Since his parents were taken away so suddenly, he was angry at God. He wasn't at peace with his friends or his acquaintances—not even with himself. He sat there for a long time and tears filled his eyes as he pleaded with Mary to show him the way to peace. In the weeks to come, he made his peace with God whom he had neglected for years. His heart was flooded with a kind of peace he had never before experienced. Tom explains his experience very briefly: "The Queen of Peace brought me to the Prince of Peace."

All of us have a longing deep within us for genuine peace. We want to be happy, contented, and fulfilled as we journey through life. We can attain this desired goal only if we are at peace with ourselves. We enjoy genuine peace of heart and mind when we are at peace with God, with others, and with creation.

We strive to be loving, kind, and gracious people. We want to be accepted, loved, and lovable. However, we experience many frustrations and failures as we try to carry out our resolve to become that kind of person. In spite of our best efforts, we see little progress in living a dedicated Christian life. We may have discovered that it is easier to be kind and gracious to the people we meet professionally and socially than to those with whom we live. We can become easily annoyed and impatient with those around us when they ask us to listen to the happenings in their lives. This is an indication that we are not at peace with ourselves. A brief inventory may help us pinpoint the areas which need our attention and healing.

- Are you content with your station in life?

- Do you decry the fact that you are not a wealthier person, able to travel far and wide for adventure?

- Are you envious of others who seem more knowledgeable and popular than you?

- Do you complain about the lack of appreciation and gratitude from members of your family and friends?

- Are you constantly reviewing your medical history, recounting your aches and pains to anyone who will listen?
- Do you find it difficult to listen patiently to others who need a listening ear and an understanding heart?
- Have you lost your sense of humor and your ability to smile?

If your answer to one or more of these questions is in the affirmative, then you are not totally at peace with yourself.

We are at peace with ourselves when we are able to accept ourselves as we are, with all our gifts and talents, with all our warts and wrinkles, with all our faults and shortcomings. We will enjoy a greater peace when we can also accept others just as they are.

Peace will reign in our hearts when we recognize the tremendous blessings the Lord has showered upon us. When we pause frequently to thank the Lord for his countless gifts and blessings, we find peace in our hearts. When we are at peace with ourselves, we smile more easily, listen more patiently, become more vitally concerned about the well-being of others. If we are at peace with ourselves, we are not easily dismayed when someone disagrees with us. Nor do we retaliate when we are criticized or insulted. Peace makes us happy, joyous people. Peace of mind and heart enables us to celebrate life with all its ups and downs. Peace removes all fears, anxieties, and worries which otherwise plague our lives and rob us of the tranquility the Lord wants us to enjoy.

Our humanness often prevents us from living up to the expectations we have for ourselves. We can readily become discouraged and frustrated. If this is your experience, then welcome to the club. There are important people in this club, such as St. Paul, the Apostle of the Gentiles. Listen to his lament: "What I do, I do not understand. For I do not do what I want, but I do what I hate." Paul continues to search for a solution and then discovers that only the Lord can help him and does come to his rescue. "Miserable one that I am! Who will deliver me from this mortal body? Thanks be to God through Jesus Christ our Lord" (Rom 7:15ff).

We can certainly identify with St. Paul, for we too do the things we do not want to do, often shattering our hope for real peace. When we alone try to transform ourselves into the kind of person we want to be, we are inviting failure. Jesus said so plainly, "Without me you can do nothing" (Jn 15:5). Since we take pride in our own accomplishments, it is difficult for us to live out this truth.

In our struggle to be at peace with ourselves at all times, we experience many failures. We ought not become discouraged, since discouragement is a powerful tool of the evil one and his favorite temptation. In our plight Jesus assures us that he knows our weaknesses, for he knows us better than we know ourselves. He comforts us with the thought that all he asks of us is a sincere effort to live in conformity with his plan in order to enjoy real peace. He knows that we want to be kind, gracious, and loving at all times. Be assured that if we fail at some point, he is there to pick us up and accompany us on our journey to the peace he wants us to enjoy in this life—a preparation for the eternal peace awaiting us.

CONFLICT

Comforting as this truth may be, we are, nonetheless, ready to ask, Why must these human weaknesses plague us in spite of our good intentions? Why can't we live as we have so frequently resolved? These honest questions deserve reflection. St. Paul sheds light on the problem of understanding ourselves when he speaks of a twofold personality within us. One he calls a natural person wounded by sin, and the other a spiritual person focusing on eternal destiny. "If there is a natural body, there is also a spiritual one" (1 Cor 15:44). Paul's explanation calls to mind the "animus" and the "anima" theory of Carl Jung. The animus is the masculine tendency within all of us to forge ahead, sometimes with little attention to detail, or much regard for the feelings of others. It is the "head" approach to all the facets of life. On the other hand, the anima is a more feminine proclivity to approach life in a more gentle, a more sensitive manner animated by the heart and soul. It has been called the divinity stirring within us. Recognizing and blending this twofold tendency will enable us to live at peace with ourselves.

We arrive at a better understanding of ourselves and of the conflicting tendencies within us—to do or not to do, to be or not to be—by recalling that we are energized by either a head or a heart approach. Both our head and our heart are striving for the same goal, but they take different routes. Seeking peace, joy, and happiness is what Carl Jung calls "humanization," meaning striving to become the best person we can possibly be.

HEAD AND HEART ON PILGRIMAGE

As we journey through life we struggle with conflicting attitudes, tendencies, responses, and actions which can rob us of the peace we desire.

The "head approach." A head approach creates a go-getter attitude urging us to travel in the fast lane. Our head reminds us that we have places to go and things to do. It usually keeps us in a hurry to prove our self-worth by striving to accomplish great things.

The head approach allows little time for reflective living or for enjoying the beauty of the people and the world around us—the blue sky and the green fields somewhat removed from the hectic freeway. We have eyes only for the fast-moving traffic, which is often too slow for us. We may even indulge in an outburst of impatience if the pace of life on our freeway slows down a mite.

The "heart approach." On the other hand, our heart represents our spiritual self. Our heart wants us to slow down, to travel the less-traveled roads through beautiful countrysides. Our heart encourages us to contemplate expansive fields and the stately trees reaching heavenward. It urges us to linger at the roadside to absorb the magnificent beauty of nature reflecting the infinite beauty of God.

Our heart reminds us of the indwelling Holy Spirit which St. Paul emphasized so frequently. He minces no words when he tells us, "Do you not know that you are the temple of God, and that the Spirit of God dwells in you" (1 Cor 3:16). Contemplating a magnificent sunset, a towering mountain, the beauty of a flower, or the smile of a child keeps us aware that the Lord is dwelling within us, empowering our eyes to see and stirring within us a deep sense of appreciation, awe, and wonder at the goodness of God.

Our head judges that we ought to go to God in times of need, but often we take little time to thank and praise him for his boundless goodness and kindness.

A FUNCTIONAL VERSUS REFLECTIVE APPROACH

Our head is concerned with functional efficiency in the happenings of the day. Our heart is attracted by the goodness and beauty in all life's events. Our head ought to take more time to discern God's will in a given situation, rather than plunging immediately into action to get things done. A functional attitude becomes mechanical and can easily depersonalize people with whom we live and interact.

The wait-and-see attitude of the heart may be called a gardener's approach. Our heart gives the seed an opportunity to germinate, mature, and produce good fruit. We are concerned about people and their welfare. The heart does not regard them as functionaries, but seeks to assist and please them. It is possible that a tension can exist between these two aspects of our personality. The head wants power, control, efficiency. The heart is more vulnerable and, recognizing its weakness, depends more on the Lord.

PRAYER POSTURES

There is a danger of dichotomy between the method of prayer proposed by the head and the heart. The head wants to be faithful to chosen prayer practices, allotting a certain amount of time to prayer each day. Following the dictates of our head, our prayers may be carefully arranged vocal prayers, such as the Rosary and other formulae of prayer. Our head finds little time for contemplation and is often filled with distractions of projects clamoring for attention, thus robbing us of precious time with the Lord who wishes to communicate with us. Our prayer may lack sincere praise and thanksgiving. Contemplative experiences may be few and fleeting.

On the other hand, when we pray with our heart, we become more reflective; these prayers are never hurried. St. Paul told us that we do not know how to pray as we ought, but to wait for the Holy Spirit to guide us in our prayer (Rom 8:26). The psalmist advises, "Leave it to the Lord and wait for him" (Ps 37:7). When we pray with our heart, we linger in the Lord's presence, aware of his love, like warm nourishing rays of the sun enveloping us. Our heart prompts us to be content to rest with the Lord in wordless prayer.

Yes, in prayer there is this difference in our approach to the Lord. These differences are not mutually exclusive. With some soul-searching and compromise, these two can blend, making us well-balanced, peaceful, and prayerful people.

Human tendencies are motivated by both head and heart. It is not a matter of choosing either the urging of our head or the prompting of our heart, but rather a reconciliation and peaceful blending of both. It would be well to spend some time alone with the Lord in a retreat or hermitage so that he may enlighten and guide us in resolving any uncertainty and lead us to the peace which is his farewell gift to us.

Prayer

Lord Jesus Christ, you said to your apostles, "I leave you peace, my peace I give you." Look not on our sins, but on the faith of your church, and grant us the peace and unity of your kingdom where you live forever and ever. [1] *Amen*

FOUR

At Peace with Others

At the time of Jesus, writing instruments were not readily available for his disciples to jot down the essence of his teaching or the teaching of the other rabbis. Nor were there recording devices to perpetuate the content of what was being said. For this reason the teachers of that day were accustomed to summarizing the essence of their teaching in a poem or short prayer which the students committed to memory, so that they could recall more easily the principal message.

Jesus summarized the moral teachings of the Old Testament by repeating:

"You shall love the Lord, your God,
with all your heart,
with all your soul, and
with all your mind."
This is the greatest and the first commandment.
The second is like it:
"You shall love your neighbor as yourself."

Matthew 22:37f

John's Gospel records how Jesus fulfilled the Old Law by proclaiming a new one: he urged us to love God as our loving Father, and to love others as he himself loves us.

Before we can establish a peaceful relationship with others, we must first have reached the two preliminary levels which Jesus mentioned: 1) peace with God by loving him as our Father, and 2) peace with ourselves by accepting ourselves as we are, letting Jesus relive his life and love in us. We are at peace with God when we try to fathom and appreciate his boundless love for us and strive to return that love by living his way of life and by accepting whatever he is pleased to send us, realizing that it is for our own sanctification. Peace is the companion and fruit of love. At times it is equated with love.

We arrive at peace with others when we try to fulfill the command Jesus gave us to love one another as he loves us (Jn 13:34). When we benevolently love another person, we are willing to accept that person as they are. We wish the best for them. Unselfish love sees the good qualities in others and helps us to recognize others as being very special to the Lord, loved by him with an infinite love. Benevolent love is accepting, helpful, kind, courteous, and gracious. Jesus gave us a powerful motive for loving another person when he told us that he would regard whatever we do for another as being done for him personally (Mt 25:40).

In the old Law or dispensation one expressed love for others by following the Golden Rule: "Do to others whatever you would have them do to you" (Mt 7:12). In the new Law of Jesus, we are asked to love others as Jesus loves us. Genuine love calls for positive action. In Tobit (4:15) we read, "Do to no one what you yourself dislike." This admonition calls only for an avoidance of anything which might be harmful to another person. Christian love, as explained by Jesus, urges us to positive action in assisting our neighbor in every possible way by our kindness and concern for them.

The commandment to love our neighbor as we love ourselves may be brief, but if we are honest, we have to admit that it causes us many problems. One reason why this law is difficult for us to put into practice is because we really do not love ourselves as we ought. We are painfully aware of all our faults and foibles, our sinfulness and infidelities. Our self-image is often very poor.

A first step in learning to be at peace with our neighbor is to be at peace with ourselves by recalling daily that the Lord loves us with an unconditional love, and that is the criterion and power of our own Christian love. He loves us just as we are, regardless of what might have happened in the past. As this conviction of mind and heart matures within us, we will be at peace with ourselves, and we will find it easier to be at peace with others. Gradually we will become aware of loving people not just with our limited, inconsistent, human love, but with the very love of God, Father, Son and Holy Spirit energizing us. This is infinitely more effective and far easier.

OBSTACLES

One of the obstacles hindering us from being at peace with others is our own insecurity. We may view others as a threat: if they seem to be more capable than we are, if they are more outgoing and make friends more easily than we do, then we will find it hard to be at peace with them.

Envy or jealousy is a hindrance to establishing a peaceful relationship with others. We can easily become envious of others with higher incomes or with fewer health problems. Others may have possessions we cannot afford, be it a better home or a newer car.

We can easily be hurt when passed over for a certain position. We may take offense at the innocent remarks of others. A major obstacle arises when someone injustly wrongs us in a real or imagined way. It is hard to relate to that person and be at peace with him. We rightly ask, *How can we love that person as Jesus commanded? How can we be at peace with him?*

Forgiveness. In our language there are a number of personal expressions which can effect a transformation within us and also within others to whom they are addressed. One of the most profound expressions is "I forgive." When someone has wronged us in any way, we ought not brood over the hurt, lest it fester within us and poison our relationship with that person. Forgiveness does not come easily to us, but again Jesus sets the example for us. The dreadful pain of his last agony on the cross was intensified by the insults, blasphemy, and ridicule leveled at him by the people he had come to save. This rejection caused him excruciating pain. Yet listen to his plea in his death agony: "Father, forgive them, for they know not what they do" (Lk 23:34).

Previously in his public ministry he often forgave sinners. He also taught us the Lord's Prayer in which we ask for forgiveness and also for the grace to forgive others, "Forgive us our debts, as we forgive our debtors" (Mt 6:12). Jesus makes forgiveness imperative as he goes on to say: "If you forgive others their transgressions, your heavenly Father will forgive you. But if you do not forgive others, neither will your Father forgive your transgressions" (Mt 6:14f).

Every time I visit a friend of mine he greets me with the words, "I forgive you everything you ever said about me." While he intends this to be humorous, it not only reminds me of the necessity of forgiveness, but it also causes me to ask myself if I had said anything unkind about him.

A LOOK AT OURSELVES

Aware of our many shortcomings, we are inclined to project our faults and weaknesses onto others. Whether or not we realize it, what we see as a defect in another person is often a reflection of our own faults and shortcomings. This realization helps us understand why we are often negative and critical of others. A critical, judgmental attitude on our part manifests a lack of peace within ourselves.

Many misunderstandings and hurts are caused by a lack of honest communications. If we would honestly and sincerely share our feelings and thoughts with one another, many strained relationships would never occur.

We can never judge another person fairly, since we cannot know the mind and heart of that individual. The Lord himself said, "More torturous than all else is the human heart, beyond remedy; who can understand it? I, the Lord, alone probe the mind and test the heart" (Jer 17:9f). As the Lord reminds us, we cannot possibly know what motivates another person's attitudes or actions. Every human being is the sum total of all his or her life's experiences. We have been influenced and shaped by every experience we have had in life. Each has helped to form our character and personality.

Let us look at a case in point. Bill has suffered rejection all the days of his life. His parents were too busy in caring for a large family to lavish love and attention on Bill as an infant. He was scarred by this rejection even though he was not aware of it. When he wanted to participate in childhood games, he was rejected. Later when he entered elementary school, he was teased and ridiculed. In adolescence he was not the brightest student, nor was he a good athlete, resulting in further rejection. Similarly, his adult life was punctuated with a number of rejections, causing him to withdraw more and more into himself. Today, Bill may be regarded as a self-centered recluse, unwilling to join in, or cooperate in social or neighborhood functions. He may seem unfriendly and little concerned about people who do not know his past experiences. We can easily become critical of his attitude without understanding what influenced his personality. How right the Lord is when he says that we cannot know the heart of another person.

PRIVILEGED GIFT

Jesus not only commanded us to love our neighbor, but also gifted us with the ability to love. He sent the Holy Spirit, the very source of divine love, to dwell within us motivating, inspiring, encouraging, and enabling us to love all who cross our path. If we are receptive to the influence of the Spirit and cooperate with his inspirations, we reflect and radiate his love, peace and joy by what we are, say, and do. The Holy Spirit enlightens and broadens our self-centered vision to recognize the goodness in others and also to appreciate their giftedness. As the fountain of peace, he fills us with his peace and assists us in establishing peaceful relationships with others.

STARTING POINT

Peaceful relationships with others are first developed in our own family. Love is the pathway to genuine peace. When children are aware of their parents' love for each other and their love for each one of them, they more easily enjoy peaceful relationships with one another. This is true even though the relationships may be strained at times.

Children will have their share of spats with their siblings. Childish whims will spark frequent little conflicts, requiring parents to be peacemakers. Such conflicts are usually transitory, causing some tension at the time, but do not disrupt the deeper peace in the family circle. I wonder if Jesus had parents in mind when he proclaimed the seventh Beatitude, "Blessed are the peacemakers..." (Mt 5:9).

When teenagers reach a rebellious age, they can upset harmony in the family. Jack and Kay, parents of three teenagers, have devised a method to restore peace when it is threatened at home. Jack put it this way, "We try to survive our teenagers by calling a family meeting around the 'peace-table.' We give each one five minutes to express his or her feelings without any interruption from anyone else, then follow up with some discussion about solutions. We can usually reach an accord that all of us can live with. On one occasion when my son, Joe, seemed to be quite obnoxious, his sister, Helen, shot back, 'If you are going to act that way, you are not my brother.' That opened the way to a calm, peaceful settlement."

When more serious disagreements are triggered in their family, Jack and Kay take the whole family to Mass to worship together and then go out for breakfast, permitting the teenagers to choose the place to eat.

Average teenagers appreciate their home and the love present there. In their years of maturing, even they are annoyed by their own rebellious reactions. I asked one teenager to jot down all his expectations of his parents. After some time he returned the blank page with the comment, "My parents are right and I have not always cooperated."

When parents' anger with their children becomes excessive, they can initiate a reconciliation by apologizing and asking forgiveness for their outburst, explaining that the children's conduct angered them, because they want them to mature into well-adjusted adults and good Christian citizens. Such an apology requires courage and humility, but it will be a powerful lesson and example for their children now and throughout the years to come.

REACHING OUT TO OTHERS

When relationships with our extended family and beyond are not highly commendable, open and honest communications can restore harmony. Usually an explanation of our feelings and actions is all that is necessary to arrive at peace with each other. The approach will certainly differ in every case, but if we ask the Lord's guidance and inspiration, he will surely assist us. If we are unwilling to attempt a reconciliation, St. Paul cautions us, "The whole law is fulfilled in one statement, namely, 'You shall love your neighbor as yourself,' but if you go biting and devouring one another, beware that you are not consumed by one another" (Gal 5:14f).

The Lord invites us to be channels through which he can radiate his love, peace, and joy to everyone in the circle in which we move. When we are at peace with God and with ourselves, we cannot conceal the peace and joy of the Lord overflowing our heart and enabling us to radiate it in our countenance, words, and actions. A friendly greeting, a quiet demeanor, an easy smile, patient listening, a gentle concern, and a willingness to assist are all ways of fulfilling the missions to which the Lord has called us. "You are the light of the world.... Just so, your light must shine before others, that they may see your good deeds and glorify your heavenly Father" (Mt 5:14ff). Our light is the love, peace, and joy we bring to others when we are at peace with them.

Prayer of St. Francis

Lord, make me an instrument of your peace;
where there is hatred, let me sow love;
where there is injury, pardon;
where there is doubt, faith;
where there is despair, hope;
where there is darkness, light; and
where there is sadness, joy.

O divine Master, grant that I may not
so much seek to be consoled as to console;
to be understood, as to understand;
to be loved, as to love;
for it is in giving that we receive,
and it is in pardoning that we are pardoned,
and it is in dying that we are born to eternal life.

FIVE

At Peace with God's Creation

I dropped in to visit Arthur, who had just retired after thirty-six years with the same company. I found him in his flower and vegetable garden—his favorite place. He told me that he never enjoyed so much peace in his life. When I suggested that perhaps it was because he had just retired and did not have to face the daily grind, he thought for a moment then replied, "That might be some of the reason, but my real peace comes from seeing the beauty in all these colorful flowers and luscious growing vegetables provided by the Lord. Just look at that tall tree. Doesn't it remind you of what Joyce Kilmer said in the poem 'Trees'—'A tree that looks at God all day and lifts her leafy arms to pray'? I often sit here in the shade absorbing all the beauty God has created. For me, that's real peace."

After we moved over to a garden bench, Arthur continued, "This is where I come every morning to spend time meditating on the goodness of the Lord in creating our earth. Look at that blue sky and those clouds lazily floating by. I call this my cathedral where I communicate with God to thank and praise him for enabling me to see and enjoy those wonderful expressions of his love." Arthur was certainly at peace with creation. My own spirits were lifted and on my way home, I noticed more carefully the trees and flowers along the way, thanks to Arthur.

All nature resonates with the beauty and love of God. The Psalms extol his creative love, "The heavens declare the glory of God, and the firmament proclaims his handiwork" (Ps 19:2). In Scripture, mountains play an important role in revealing some of God's attributes. Mountains are often the meeting place of God with his people. On Mt. Sinai God revealed his providential care and his law; on Mt. Tabor Jesus radiated his divinity shining through his humanity; on the rock of Calvary, Jesus proved that there is no greater love than to lay down his life for his friends.

The majestic beauty of the towering mountains reaching heavenward readily elevates our minds and hearts to the God of creation. Their lofty pinnacles inspire awe and admiration, moving us into a reflective mood and into prayer. The rugged beauty of the mountains reminds us of the power and care of a God who is our Father. This awareness enkindles within us awe and reverence, peace, and joy.

We need not go far afield to become aware of the goodness and beauty reflected in all the works of creation. He created our bodies with agility, enabling us to perform countless functions. We can work, play, walk, run. The dexterity of our hands gives us the ability to perform endless tasks and various functions. Our hands help us to communicate our feelings of admiration and affection for another person. Likewise a gesture reveals rejection or disgust for a person.

Even a passing reflection on the intricacies of God's works of creation reveals his boundless love for us. Such a reflection keeps us aware of his infinite love—the pathway to and the basis of peace.

CREATION IS ONGOING

In Scripture we read that when God finished creating the world in six days, "He looked at everything he had made and found it very good" (Gn 1:31). God did not stop creating after the sixth day, nor is creation complete. God is continually creating and re-creating; it is an ongoing process.

At a social gathering one evening, a well-known obstetrician was asked if he believed in miracles. With a gracious smile he responded, "I see them every day." In his practice he regarded the birth of every baby as a special creation of God.

Every spring of the year we witness the re-creation of the new buds, blossoms, and leaves sprouting on trees and plants. Early flowers lift their faces for our admiration and enjoyment.

God also creates and re-creates in less dramatic ways. If we cut a finger, immediately new cells are being created to replace damaged cells and heal the wound.

St. Paul speaks of a spiritual re-creation when he reminds us that for our sake Christ died and was raised "so whoever is in Christ is a new creation" (2 Cor 5:17).

HUMAN LIMITATIONS

Because of our human condition, we are restricted in many different ways. But with God's help, if we are able to accept our human frailties and limitations, we can enjoy great peace.

To achieve certain goals in life, we need to acquire sufficient knowledge to equip ourselves for certain tasks. Reading and study bring satisfaction and enjoyment and lead us into peace. We may not be as talented as another person, but humble acceptance of that fact helps make us a peaceful people nonetheless. When I asked a sixth-grade boy about his report card, he said: "I am not very smart, but I try to be good." He seemed at peace with his mental capacity.

Limited physical strength and stamina may prevent us from accomplishing all the feats we long to attain—a perfect golf score, winning a foot race, climbing a mountain. A peaceful person does not become impatient or regret these limitations, but recognizes and appreciates the countless other gifts and blessings from the Lord.

Illness is an acid test of our humanness. Temporary illness may force us to postpone or cancel carefully planned programs and projects. The ability to do so without complaint or frustration is a sure road to peace. It may require considerable time to make necessary adjustments and change our attitude, but eventual acceptance brings peace.

Longer illness or physical impairment, especially one which means much dependence on others, requires an adjustment of major proportions. The abiding presence of Jesus with us, and the peace he shares with us, supports us in making difficult adjustments. We are deeply impressed and edified by persons who endure great pain and hardship, and yet radiate a joy and peace which only the Lord can give. They make our own little problems seem so insignificant.

PARAGON

Jesus never asks us to do anything or to accept any suffering which he himself has not endured. In all the happenings in his life, Jesus showed us the way. On several occasions Jesus became tired and weary. On his way back to Galilee, he became so tired he had to sit down at Jacob's well to rest while the disciples went off to buy food (Jn 4:6). On another occasion, after he had taught and healed all day, he was exhausted. Mothers brought their children that he might lay his hands on them and bless them. The disciples tried to protect him by stopping the people from bringing their children to him. Jesus did not complain, pity himself nor excuse himself. On the contrary, he chided his disciples, "Let the children come to me, and do not prevent them" (Mt 19:13ff). Jesus also experienced the pain of rejection, desertion, and betrayal by chosen friends. He did not indulge in self-pity. From the Garden of Gethsemane and throughout the treacherous judgments, scourging, crowning with thorns, and final oblation on the cross, Jesus uttered no reproach and kept his will attuned to the will of the Father. His love for us sustained him through it all, making him the model in helping us to accept our humanness.

AVENUES TO PEACE

An easy and effective means of keeping ourselves aware of God's creative love is through our external senses—momentary pauses to remind ourselves that what we see, hear, smell, touch, or taste are experiences of God. Practically every television program is punctuated with numerous commercials, much to our distress at times. If we would develop the habit of interspersing our daily duties with ten- or thirty-second pauses to remind ourselves that God is present all around us, we would experience the peaceful presence and power of the Lord with us at all times.

Most of us experience life as a driver or passenger dashing down the freeways at high speed. We take little time to observe, study, or appreciate the sights and scenes passing by. On the other hand, we can develop the habit of pausing to enjoy a magnificent sunset, the beauty of a rose, the presence of a loved one, the smile of a child. Awareness of the Lord's creative presence brings us much peace.

Listening with our heart is vitally important, because we cannot know a person to whom we do not listen, nor can we love a person we do not know. We cannot appreciate the sounds of God around us, unless we listen. The gift of hearing enables us to experience the creative presence of God in sounds we hear— in conversations, in the song of a bird, in good music, in the whispering pines, in the sound of silence.

The fragrance of flowers, the freshness of the early morning air, the tempting aroma of freshly perked coffee and newly baked bread can remind us of the goodness of the Lord. Our gift of smell can encourage us to turn to the Lord for a prayerful moment.

What delight our sense of taste brings! We satisfy hunger and quench thirst with this gift of God's creative love. A delectable meal ought to inspire us to thank the Lord for the favorable climate that produces the food we eat and for the people who planted, harvested, transported, and prepared it for us. Taste continually reminds us of the providential love and goodness of the Lord, the source of peace.

We can sacramentalize each of the thousand objects we touch throughout the course of the day by permitting them to remind us of the Lord. We need to sensitize ourselves to the fact that all we touch and all that touches us is the creative work and design of the Father. How healing a hug can be when pain or sorrow pierces our heart! The firm handshake of a friend speaks to us of loving concern or of support in what we have done or are endeavoring to do. A breeze can waft away weariness after hard work. The litany goes on indefinitely, since we touch so many objects each day.

External senses can and do bring us into deeper awareness of what God has created for us. Each work of God's creation speaks of his boundless love for us. Knowing his love at the very depth of our being will keep us at peace with all creation.

God's gift of peace, which the world cannot give, will sustain us and enable us to survive whatever losses come our way in life.

Prayer

Loving Father, you created all things for our sustenance and enjoyment. You endowed us, your creatures, with a potential to receive your divine life, partially in this life, but in all its fullness for an eternity of heavenly bliss with you. "Let all your works give you thanks, O God, and let your faithful ones bless you" (Ps 145:10). Amen

SECTION II

———◆———

Finding God in the Seasons and Circumstances of Life

SIX

Faith Crisis

In the world today there is a growing tendency to abandon Christian beliefs and practices, a trend that has created a widespread crisis in faith. This crisis has invaded many of our homes and spread throughout our country and the world. This is tragic, for without a strong, living faith the results are obvious: people are confused and fearful, their lives unfulfilled, lacking meaning and purpose. They find little peace, joy, and contentment in their lives.

WHAT IS FAITH?

Faith is a free gift of God empowering us to say "Yes, I believe" to God in whatever he teaches, and then commit ourselves to live according to the way of life he has mapped out for us. Faith is a firm belief in God and in the divine truths he has revealed. It is an implicit trust in his divine providence hovering over us at all times. Faith is the firm conviction that God loves us with an unconditional, immutable love, regardless of who we are or what we may have done in our lives. In his Word, the Spirit tells us, "Faith is the realization of what is hoped for and evidence of things unseen." It also cautions us: "But without faith it is impossible to please God" (Heb 11:1,6).

The gift of faith is given to us like a tiny seed. We are to cultivate, nurture, and care for that seed, enabling it to grow and mature into a vibrant, dynamic faith in God. To cause that seed of faith to develop, we must establish a deep personal relationship with the Lord, realizing that he loves us with an unconditional love. As we become more and more aware of his love for us, it will elicit a love response within us. As our love for the Lord increases, our faith likewise will increase.

Faith engenders a trust and confidence in God even though we cannot clearly see his will in all that he asks of us. Scripture reminds us, "At present we see indistinctly, as in a mirror, but then face to face" (1 Cor 13:12). Again Scripture tells us that faith is a gift of God freely given, without which we could not be saved. "For by grace you have been saved through faith, and this is not from you; it is the gift of God; it is not from works" (Eph 2:8). That seed of faith lies dormant within us, waiting for us to be receptive and cooperative in helping it to develop into a genuine, committed faith.

Today we are witnessing an ever-growing trend, especially among young people, to abandon the Lord and to give up practicing a Christian way of life. We may speak of people losing their faith, but this statement is not totally accurate. Some are struggling with fears and doubts arising within them concerning certain truths and practices which they do not understand. For others, when their expectations have not been met, they conclude that God is not interested in them and their problems. Still others are exposed to various false theories being propounded in lecture halls or by their peers. These people have not lost their gift of faith, but it has been weakened or lies dormant.

Ginny had just returned home after completing her third year in college as a psychology major. It was a delightful reunion for the whole family. When plans were being made to attend Mass on Sunday, Ginny shyly announced that she would not be going to Mass. She explained that in her classes they were taught that the Bible is misrepresented and is not very accurate, and that many of the Church's teachings are intended to control. It was a shock to the family, especially to her parents.

REASONS FOR THE LOSS OF FAITH

As we reflect on some of the social trends of our times, it becomes quite evident how pernicious are many of the influences in our lives. Many of them are responsible for the crisis in faith and the straying away from the Lord. A brief reflection on some of the causes may clarify some of the doubts and misgivings that cause faith to wane.

Lack of knowledge. There is a woeful misunderstanding and lack of knowledge about the Church and her teachings. Some regard the Church as an establishment dictating rules and regulations that curtail our self-indulgent freedom. Seldom do they realize that the Church is the Body of Christ in which we are privileged members called by the Lord himself through our Baptism to enjoy all the gifts and blessings he wishes to shower upon us through the sacramental system, especially through the Holy Eucharist. Someone put it in these words, "There is a wholesale illiteracy about the Church and her teachings."

One man I know expounds without hesitation on his reasons—mostly rationalizations—why he does not go to church or practice a Christian way of life. He maintains that all the Church wants is his money, and then gives his final reason, "Priests are leaving, why shouldn't I?" After a brief conversation with David, it is quite evident that he knows very little about the Lord's teaching as set forth by the Church. Unfortunately, in his younger years he did not have the good fortune of learning very much about the Catholic faith.

Transition. Our age is a time of great transition in which our understanding of God as a gracious Father is changing. Formerly, we envisioned God as an avenging God, ready to punish the least infraction of his law. We considered ourselves good Christians if we obeyed all his mandates. While this is true, our motivation was a fear of punishment if we did not observe all the Lord's commandments.

Today our understanding of God is formed not so much by our intellect as a desire to know him with our hearts as a personal, kind Father who loves us with a boundless love. Experiencing his love in a deeper, more personal way will motivate us to respond to his love by striving to do everything to please him out of a sense of love rather than legalism. When we really love a person, we want to do everything to please that person. When we love God, we try to live his way of life with an earnest dedication. Jesus said, "Whoever has my commandments and observes them is the one who loves me" (Jn 14:21).

Age of technology. In this age of technology we have made some wonderful strides in making life more convenient and comfortable. Unfortunately, the mentality that it has produced in some people has taken its toll on their faith. We have become a proud, sophisticated people. Some of our technological discoveries have made us feel so self-sufficient that we have little time for God. Likewise, our intellectual knowledge has increased so rapidly in the last few generations that we pride ourselves on being able to solve all the secrets of nature by simply touching the right key on the computer. In the near future we hope to solve all mysteries of our religion. Our achievements in space travel are indeed commendable, but while we hail man's ability to accomplish these tremendous feats, it has taken a toll on many people by weakening their faith in the Creator and Sustainer of the whole universe. When we pride ourselves on our intellectual achievements, we may become oblivious to the fact that God has given us the very gifts and talents we use so gratuitously to explore his marvelous creation.

Instead of promoting pride in ourselves, all these magnificent accomplishments should deepen our faith in God and inspire us to praise and glorify him for all he does for us.

Edward was an intelligent and successful young businessman with a beautiful wife and two young children. He was a proud young man and boasted of his business acumen that enabled him to amass a comfortable fortune in just a few years. He wanted to discuss some important questions with me. He asked me to prove conclusively that the words attributed to Jesus at the Last Supper, when he instituted the Eucharist, are the very words that Jesus himself spoke. Furthermore, he wanted some intellectual proof that the Lord is really present in the Eucharist and that he commanded us to continue to offer the Eucharist. Or, he asked, was this merely a regulation of the Church? Other questions flowed from him for which he wanted straightforward answers.

When he finished, I did not say a word. Knowing Edward since he was a boy, I felt that I could be forthright with him. When the pause was getting uncomfortable, I told him that I could not give him the kind of proof he was seeking. I told him that whatever proof I would offer, he would reject because he was not open and would therefore voice further objections. I explained to him that we approach God with faith in him and in the mysteries he revealed to us. I tried to show him that with our human intellect we cannot fathom the mystery of God. Reason will never replace our faith. I was fearful that I might alienate him totally, yet I had to move him away from the proud stance he had taken. Before he left he asked if he could come back to see me again.

I knew that Edward had not been going to Mass with his family and that he was trying to convince his wife that he had no obligation to go since he did not have definitive proof for the Eucharist. He was also trying to rationalize his conviction that his actions were justified. His success in the business world had made him a very proud, self-sufficient person lacking humility which generates and strengthens faith.

Peer pressure. Peer pressure, accompanied with its subtle persecution, contributes to the weakening of faith in some people. As we endeavor to live a dedicated Christian life, we can expect to be criticized and ridiculed by our peers. We may be called old-fashioned and advised to catch up with the modern trends. Jesus warned us that we would be persecuted as he was (Jn 15:20).

George had to drop out of his golf foursome when their tee time was changed to Sunday morning. Several snide remarks were leveled at him by his friends. At his work, Joe overheard some derogatory comments when he refused to be amused by their off-color jokes. Arlene, a wonderful mother of four, is continually being reminded that her family is twice the size of what an average American family should be. She was laughed at more than once when she could not accept invitations to go out to golf with her friends, or attend their luncheons or other social events.

When we experience these comments and attitudes daily from various sources, it may cause us to question our own faith-walk, or raise some doubts and misgivings in our own hearts. Eventually it can weaken our faith. Many of those in our materialistic society ignore God and his way of life. When we are bombarded by these attitudes, our faith can suffer.

Bob's faith was on the wane. He maintained that the Lord was not fair to him. He worked hard but mounting medical bills and other expenses kept him from providing for his family as he wanted. He envied his friends and neighbors who seemed to be better off. His wife tried to convince him that his faith and trust in the providence of God was weakening, which he vehemently denied.

One day as he watched his wife lifting their four-month-old daughter high in the air and swinging her to and fro, he noticed that the infant showed no sign of fear. On the contrary, she cooed and gurgled with delight. *What confidence and trust!* Bob thought.

He recalled that when their older son was learning to walk, he took his first staggering steps toward the outstretched arms of his father without any show of fear. The toddler took these few faltering steps with confidence and trust that his father would rescue him. And now, a few years later, his son was at his knee asking him to fix his toy. He was confident that his daddy could do anything. As Bob fixed the toy with a few manipulations, a light dawned on him. If his children had so much faith and trust in their parents, why should he not have that same faith and trust in God?

At this early stage in life, children may not understand anything about the gift of faith, but they place their trust in their parents because they know somehow that they are loved. Mothers and fathers become the avenue which will eventually lead their children to an operative, dynamic faith.

Jesus urges us to have the heart of a child with a simple, trusting faith. Our heavenly Father also wishes us to have a childlike faith in him and trust him implicitly in all the happenings of life.

When Jesus walked the face of the earth, he begged consistently for faith in himself and in all the teachings he proclaimed. When he found genuine faith, he was greatly pleased. On the other hand, when faith in him was lacking, he was obviously deeply disappointed. The Gospel records a pathetic incident that took place in his hometown of Nazareth. When he returned to Nazareth, the people did not believe in him; they rejected him. Scripture relates this tragic event, "He did not work many mighty deeds there because of their lack of faith" (Mt 13:58).

Jesus is the same yesterday, today, and always (Heb 13:8). He is operative within our lives, and asks us to have faith in him. Perhaps he may be prevented from working wonders in our lives because of our lack of vibrant faith in him.

LEVELS OF FAITH

The first level of faith is an intellectual assent to a truth that has been clearly revealed, but one which we cannot understand. This is the lowest level of faith. The mystery of the Blessed Trinity is one example. It has been revealed in Scripture, giving us some insights into this marvelous truth, but still it is incomprehensible to our finite minds.

The second level of faith is called the faith of commitment. When we reach this level of faith we are willing to commit ourselves to some special calling, project, or program. Every good marriage is based on the faith of commitment, as is also the vowed life. When we believe that God is calling us to some special work or vocation and we embrace it as the will of the Lord, we are living our faith of commitment.

The next level of faith is known as the faith of expectancy. With this level of faith, we confidently feel, know, believe and trust that God will act in every situation in our lives. We know that he cares for us and that his love is so extravagant that he will never permit anything to happen to us from which we cannot draw some good. This level of faith is pleasing to God. It is the level to which we are all called. As we pray for a deepening of our faith, the Lord will become the first priority in our lives, and we will live with this expectant faith which is so pleasing to the Lord.

INCREASING OUR FAITH

Faith is a divine gift eagerly and freely given to anyone prepared to receive it. We must cherish and nurture it by using well this privileged gift. We keep ourselves receptive for a continual increase in faith by expressing our appreciation for the Lord's marvelous gift so freely given. Praising and thanking God for our gift of faith will keep us humble and more willing to trust him implicitly, come what may.

Our constant prayer should be a fervent petition for the Lord's help to make our faith vibrant, dynamic, unwavering. Following the example of the father of the possessed boy, our prayer can be brief, but repeated frequently, "I do believe, help my unbelief!" (Mk 9:24).

Our faith level is enriched every time we accept and go forward in any circumstance that may arise, knowing that the Lord is with us to guide, encourage, and strengthen us in all our decisions and actions. The higher our level of trust, the more pleasing to the Lord.

OUR CALL TO A FAITH-WALK

Each one of us has a tremendous potential to counteract the decline of faith so rampant around us. A dynamic, fervent faith will solve many of the problems facing us today and even help to avoid the many tragic happenings in our country and in the world.

The dynamic of faith must begin with each one of us on a personal level. If our faith is strong and vibrant, our whole lifestyle will reflect our trust and confidence in God's providential care. Without being aware of it, we will radiate our faith-filled attitudes and convictions to others.

At this juncture, we may be tempted to say that we are only one person in this whole wide world—what influence do we have? How much of an impact can we have on other people?

If we live by faith and if we influence one other person each month and that person in turn strengthens the faith in one other person each month, by geometric progression we will have touched 4,000 people annually. With God's help, we can make a difference.

The Holy Spirit encourages us in our endeavors when he assures us, "And the victory that conquers the world is our faith" (1 Jn 5:4).

Prayer

Lord Jesus, you urged us to have faith in the Father and faith in you. Grant me the gift of vibrant, expectant faith in all the happenings in life. May my prayer always be, "I do believe, help my unbelief." Amen

SEVEN

Daily Burdens

A monk who was usually cheerful and outgoing seemed to be depressed. He communicated very little and spent much time alone. He went about his routine duties without much enthusiasm. When this became apparent to many others, the abbot asked what in particular was bothering him and if he could be any help. The monk replied, "Nothing in particular but the whole darned business." Little doubt that this good monk has lots of company. Do we not find ourselves in a similar situation? The drudgery of each day can become monotonous and frustrating. Life can become a series of duties, demands, and difficulties with one hardship following on the heels of the previous one. These demands seem all the more burdensome because they leave us little time to do what we would like to do. The very fact that we cannot do the things we want seems to make them all the more desirable—the ideal escape from demanding duties of the day.

Furthermore, even if we are faithful in trying to do all that is expected of us, no one seems to appreciate or thank us, or even notice what we do. We get weary and often do not feel well, yet no one seems to be concerned. Our daily duties do not seem to be gratifying challenges for us anymore. These are some of the ordinary tasks which plague us. If we allow a negative attitude to take hold of us, our misery and unhappiness intensifies. Countless people rise above such sentiments only by taking their eyes off the immediate circumstances and looking for a larger purpose.

CIRCUMSTANTIAL BURDENS

A brief survey will demonstrate to us that people in different walks of life are faced with burdens of various kinds. Edna's infant son calls for attention several times during the night, denying her a restful sleep. She wards off self-pity by reminding herself that her own mother must have surely gotten up many times to care for her when she was an infant.

Will battles traffic on his way to work for forty minutes each morning and evening. He calls this his prayer time since he listens to tapes recounting the gospel message and chats with the Lord, his front-seat passenger. Will also confesses that at times his conversation is not always the most uplifting when the traffic gets snarled.

A young refugee in our country spends long, tedious hours each day with a dictionary close at hand, studying to improve his education. Even though he also works several hours a week for low wages, leaving him little time for recreation, he has maintained his place on the honor roll.

Jill and Pat had to cancel their planned weekend trip to the children's grandparents when one of the children became ill. When Pat called his mother to inform her that they were unable to come, he told her, "Man proposes but God disposes." This reminder helped to avoid disappointment and self-pity. Even a casual observation of the trials and difficulties others endure will enable us to rise above discouragement or depression.

INTERPERSONAL BURDENS

Some interpersonal relationships can be a burden to us. Joyce's neighbor is a friendly person who pops in at the most inopportune times—usually while her children are taking over the yard for their games. Since she is well-intentioned and otherwise a gracious person, there is little that Joyce can say or do but bear the burden quietly. She also thanks God that it is not a neighbor who is obnoxious and hostile, or a late-night party-loving neighbor who manages to keep the neighborhood awake until the wee hours, or a neighbor with a friendly dog who cries for attention throughout the night and greets people with a sonorous bark during the day.

PARENT-CHILDREN CONFLICTS

Burdens arise from various sources in our daily living. One of the burdens for parents is the challenge their teenagers throw in their path. The period of adolescence is a confusing time for both young people and parents alike. Teenagers' moods and foibles are unpredictable, causing little crises to arise at any given moment.

When we feel ourselves becoming angry with our children, we ought to defuse our anger before we vent it on our offspring so vehemently that we have only regrets afterwards.

We can calm our anger by taking a shower, going for a brisk walk, or just taking "time out" after we have explained to the "culprit" that we need to calm down and will deal with the problem later. Such a method can be effective for the child also, giving him an opportunity to reflect on his role in causing the misunderstanding or disturbance.

REFRESHING PAUSE

When life seems storm-tossed and we are inundated by the threatening waves of disappointments and pains, the Gospel episode of the disciples attempting to cross the stormy Sea of Galilee has a special message for us (Jn 6:16ff). The disciples were rowing vigorously with the hope of reaching their destination, Capernaum, on the other side of the lake. Strong winds thwarted all their efforts, causing them to fear for their lives. Suddenly Jesus appeared, walking toward them on the water, to reassure them and bring them to the shore of Capernaum, their destination.

This same Jesus is walking at our side, eager to assist us, to allay our fears, to bring us comfort, and to lighten our burden by assuming most of the load. Moreover, he assures us that our suffering need not be in vain, but can condition us so that he may work more fully in and through us. He gives us new insights into suffering, lays his hand on our feverish brow, gives us a pat on the back to reassure us that we are his good and faithful servant. This is what he meant when he told us that he would be with us always, and never leave us orphans.

LONG-TERM BURDENS

God calls some of his friends to a special ministry close to his heart. This can be a taxing, long-term, time-consuming burden, but it has sanctifying power and rewarding love. Willing acceptance of this burden paves the road to heaven and brings us much satisfaction.

These special friends of the Lord are people called to care for the infirm, the elderly, and the disabled, as the Lord himself did during his earthly sojourn. They are the mothers and fathers who lovingly care for a sickly or handicapped child; or a son or daughter, husband or wife caring for an aging or helpless par-

ent or spouse. Medical professionals have a unique commission
from the Lord to offer their skills and services to the sick and
needy, especially the elderly and disabled.

Long-term caregiving, even when lovingly and cheerfully
shouldered, is emotionally draining and exhausting, especially
when we experience a loved one suffering. In some cases, this
ministry is a nonstop, twenty-four-hour, seven-day-a-week
commitment. This special calling to care for the infirm is close
to the heart of the Lord. Jesus always manifested a loving concern for the sick and suffering. He always reached out to comfort and console, and in most cases to heal them. The Lord
also has a special predilection for all who care for the elderly
and the suffering.

In Matthew's Gospel, Jesus was pleased with the father who
trustingly brought his afflicted son to him and, with great faith,
begged for a healing (Mt 17:14ff). The Canaanite woman
risked rejection since she was not a Jew, but perseveringly
pleaded for her daughter's healing (Mk 7:24ff). Jesus was visi-
bly pleased when a Roman centurion cared enough about his
dying servant that he overcame his pride and approached Jesus
for healing (Mt 8:5ff). St. Luke makes clear that Jesus was
greatly gratified when the four men carried a paralytic on a
stretcher to ask for healing. We do not know how far they carried him, but Jesus was very much pleased with their faith and
the extraordinary efforts they made to place the paralytic before
him (Lk 5:17ff). These were all caring people who, forgetful of
self, made great sacrifices to be of service to the helpless and
needy.

In the account of the Last Judgment, Jesus specifically
points out services offered to others and mentions the positive
works of charity for which a person will "inherit the kingdom
prepared from the foundation of the world" (Mt 25:34).
Listed among the overt works of charity is caring for those who
are infirm; for example, "I was ill and you cared for me" is an
act of love for which we will receive eternal life. Jesus concludes

by explaining why this service is so meritorious: "Amen, I say to you, whatever you did for one of these least brothers of mine, you did it for me" (See Mt 25:31ff).

If we are willing to accept a burden of suffering laid upon us, or are striving to assume cheerfully the burden of caring for another, but in the process we become weary and impatient, or even question the Lord's love, we are not unfaithful servants. We are only human and our human nature rebels from time to time. The Lord uses these occasions and trials to teach us to depend more upon him and to grow in our relationship with him.

NEVER ALONE

When our burdens seem overwhelming and we are tempted to become discouraged and frustrated, Jesus reminds us, "Without me you can do nothing." There is a positive ring in this caution, for the Lord is assuring us that with him we can do all things. Turning to him for help will lift our spirits and lighten every burden. When weariness, fatigue and discouragement beset us, the Lord invites us, "Come to me, all you who labor and are burdened, and I will give you rest.... For my yoke is easy and my burden light" (Mt 11:28ff).

In Israel I watched an Arab farmer preparing the soil for planting using an ancient plow drawn by a team made up of a camel and a donkey. The long strides of the camel made it almost impossible for the donkey to keep pace. He had to take more and quicker steps to keep up with the long strides of the camel and keep the traces taut. Despite his best efforts he was pulling a smaller part of the load. As I watched this, the words of Jesus came to mind with a new clarity. We are yoked to the Lord at all times. Like the camel, he pulls the greatest part of our load and lifts much of our burden; he asks only that we make an effort to keep pace with him and his plans for us.

ATTITUDINAL ADJUSTMENT

The surest way to find peace and fulfillment in accepting and enduring our burdens is to offer each one as a special love-offering to the Lord, for the benefit of the person we are assisting. When motivated by love, we carry our burdens more tolerably and even with joy. It was his insatiable love for us that brought Jesus to the cross. "No one has greater love than this, to lay down one's life for one's friends" (Jn 15:13). Ever since, his admonition has been re-echoing down the centuries.

Victor Herbert's "Ah Sweet Mystery of Life" reminds us: "For 'tis love and love alone, the world is seeking."[1] A popular logo used by Father Flannagan's Boys' Town depicts a lad carrying another young boy piggyback with the caption, "He ain't heavy, Father, he's my brother."

When love is our motivating force, we can more easily detect the silver lining in every cloud. We discover that the sun is shining more brilliantly, making our burdens seem much lighter. The Lord blesses our willingness to accept the burdens that come our way. Love also helps us to recognize each burden as a stepping stone into closer union with the Lord.

Prayer

Lord Jesus, thank you for calling me to this special mission so close to your heart. Strengthen me to fulfill my calling faithfully and reflect your loving concern to the special person entrusted to my care. Help me to accept each burden as together we journey down life's highway until we reach our heavenly home with you. Amen

EIGHT

What God Has Joined Together

After nearly thirty years of married life, Kathleen felt she just had to talk to someone or she would explode. Even though on the surface her marriage seemed to be going well, Kathleen was tormented with the feeling that something was missing in her relationship with her husband. They communicated on the surface about the happenings in their daily routine, but her husband, Bob, was oblivious of her longing for deeper communication and for real intimacy and joy. She felt that he was cold and indifferent to her feelings. When she tried to explain to Bob her feelings of "something missing," he became confused and angry. He demanded to know what more she expected of him. He reminded her that he was providing well for the family, and that he was a good father to the children and a faithful husband. What else did she want from him? As the conflict continued, it grew in intensity and drove them farther apart. Kathleen asked herself if a divorce was a way out. Could she find more peace of mind away from her husband?

77

CONFLICTS

Problems, misunderstandings, frustrations, and conflicts are all part and parcel of our human condition. Given our broken human nature, we can expect conflicts to arise from time to time. In married life it is inevitable that when two people live in such a close relationship, rubbing elbows every day, conflicts will arise. Some couples are afraid that conflicts are a threat to their mutual relationship. On the contrary, true intimacy cannot happen unless we are able to deal openly and honestly with our feelings.

I know a couple who pride themselves on the fact that they have never had a conflict—not even a serious argument—in all their thirty-six years of married life. It is obvious to all their friends that the husband is a forceful, domineering person. Throughout the years his wife has always taken flight by denying her feelings, always accepting and submitting to her husband's wishes and demands just to keep peace and harmony in their household. It is quite apparent that this is not genuine love, but a flight before oncoming self-centered love. Mature love enables us to share our feelings honestly, to listen attentively, and to compromise willingly in order to reach a mutual accord and "serve one another through love" (Gal 5:13).

CONFLICTS INEVITABLE: A REALITY OF LIFE

As we journey down the pathway of life, conflicts will naturally arise at almost every turn in the road. They are seldom avoidable, especially in the intimacy of married life. Disagreements will arise on a variety of matters, such as disciplining children, money matters, social visits and visiting in-laws, drinking, household chores, the possibility of moving into another house, buying a new car, and a multiplicity of other problems.

When Ruth expressed her desire to get a job, Jeff immediately got very angry. He accused Ruth of deserting him and neglecting the children. He simply would not hear of it. Ruth was terribly upset because Jeff would not even listen when she tried to tell him that she wanted to use her talents and also to be able to lay away money for the children's education. Jeff countered that he would be greatly humiliated among his friends since it would appear to them that he was not adequately providing for his family. He suggested that Ruth's working might endanger their marriage. Jeff reminded his wife of the marriages that are destroyed when a working woman falls in love with a co-worker. This hurt Ruth very deeply.

It is obvious that married life is not always moonlight and roses. Problems are unavoidable when two people live in such close proximity. When a major change is necessitated in the lifestyle of a family, it is frequently the cause of a conflict. Few people welcome change, which often threatens their security. The changes that take place in married life come in many different forms: a wife going back to work, a newborn baby arriving, the loss of employment, a transfer requiring a move to a distant city, an elderly parent moving in, or simply the chaos associated with our children's teenage years.

Every major change requires a bundle of patience and loads of goodwill, considerable personal sacrifice and some difficult adjustments. Without these, husband and wife can burn up a lot of emotional energy, resulting in frayed nerves that take their toll on their relationship. If they do not take time to discuss openly and respectfully a creative approach to the difficulties which change requires, it can cause serious damage in their relationship.

John and Pam were all excited about their first baby. John loved the little infant dearly. However, as the months rolled by, John felt neglected as all Pam's interest, time, and energy was absorbed in caring for their newborn. He felt he hardly got a passing notice. This feeling fermented within him for some time until he was honest enough to admit it to himself and to Pam. Together they made an adjustment in their relationship to one another and to the change in their lifestyle.

In marriage, conflicts can be either destructive or beneficial, depending on how a couple reacts to the problem and to each other. It is similar to approaching a fork in the road. We can choose one direction, which could bring us safely to an amicable solution, or we may choose the other path which could lead us into more confusion, get us lost in controversy, and cause greater stress and pain.

When a serious disagreement arises, couples may react in negative ways which will not resolve the crisis. One or both may flee the scene of combat, leave the house, retreat into frigid silence, shed tears, or make light of a situation deserving serious attention.

Another devastating response is abusive language, endless quarreling, and shouting at each other. Fighting only wounds more deeply and solves nothing. Conflicts should not be a "win-lose" situation but a "win-win" agreement. Ideally, husbands and wives who listen sympathetically and try to understand the other person's feelings not only arrive at a mutually agreeable solution, but will grow and mature in their love for each other.

COPING WITH CONFLICT

How best can differences of opinion be resolved and peace restored to a household? The spouse who first attempts to resolve a crisis should be commended. This is not a manifestation of guilt or weakness but a sign of genuine strength. It takes courage and humility to initiate a reconciliation.

A good rule when an eruption occurs is never to let the disagreement linger or wait too long to make up. Sacred Scripture sets forth a good principle to follow: "Be angry, but do not sin; do not let the sun go down on your anger, and do not leave room for the devil" (Eph 4:26f). A good rule for a couple is never to go to sleep at night before making up. If the hurts drag on, anger and resentment will build up, resulting in self-pity and making a resolution even more difficult.

Pent-up angry feelings can be explosive. They fester beneath the surface and eventually poison not only a person's thinking but the whole marital relationship. If a husband or wife vents anger, the other spouse needs to recognize the feelings, sympathize, and try to see some truth in what is being said.

Mike realized that Connie had some pent-up emotions which kept her on edge for several days. One morning at breakfast he asked if there was anything he could do. His question triggered an angry response from Connie, who informed him that nothing was wrong. When he left for work the tension was high and the atmosphere heavy. Connie became more upset when he did not call during the day as he usually did. That evening when Mike arrived home from work he told Connie that he was taking the next day off so they could spend it together and do some of the things she liked to do. Needless to say, it was a great healing day.

Attempting to justify one's position by trying to prove the other person wrong will certainly cause more hurt and angry feelings. We do well to remind ourselves that one person is never totally right and the other person never entirely wrong. In the midst of a heated disagreement, insulting language is destructive and completely out of place. Name-calling and dredging up past grievances impede any steps toward agreement or compromise. Physical abuse is never to be tolerated.

In every situation, the other person deserves our respect. We need to listen with an open mind and heart. If we really hear not only the words, but what the other person is trying to say, we would see that he or she has good insights and valid reasons. Receptive minds and hearts can solve the strongest disagreements. Likewise, as we listen we can better sort out the real issues by trying to discover points on which we can agree and then begin to compromise.

Bill and Julie worked out their own plan to deal with any problem, difference of opinion, or conflict which may arise in their marriage. They choose a quiet, unhurried time to resolve a disagreement in this way. Sometimes Julie takes the first step.

She has ten minutes to express her feelings and opinions without any interruption. Bill may not ask any questions, make any rebuttal, or discuss any part of Julie's presentation. Next Bill has equal time to verbalize his ideas, feelings or thoughts. Following the same procedure, Julie may not make any comments or ask any questions or offer any explanation. The meeting is then adjourned for a whole day to give them time to reflect and digest what was said. The next day, at a convenient time, they come together to discuss their reflections and try to discern what the Lord would want them to do in this particular case. A peaceful solution is nearly always found and they are able to continue their journey together.

COUNSELING

When a major conflict looms, seek some counseling before it becomes a full-blown crisis. A good Christian counselor can be helpful in many difficult situations. Some couples prefer to seek help from a clergyman who is knowledgeable and competent in this area.

Some married persons hesitate to seek counseling because they believe it gives the impression that their lives and their marriage are a failure. Others resent the suggestion of counseling because they do not want to reveal their own private lives, or their own convictions may be threatened. We need to be reminded that when we are suffering physically, we do not hesitate to see a doctor to seek relief. Emotional suffering can be even more painful and can bring disastrous consequences. Professional help can mean not only survival but even a peaceful solution.

In some cases one or two counseling sessions may be sufficient to alert couples to the real problem and guide them toward a peaceful resolution of the problem. A Swedish proverb reminds us that when we share a joy, we increase our own joy; when we share a sorrow, it will halve our distress.

When we hear ourselves verbalize our feelings and opinions, we can get a deeper insight into the problem and get a better understanding of the cause of the conflict, enabling us to arrive at a solution.

THE MAGIC OF "I'M SORRY"

A cartoon portrayed a husband saying to his wife, "There are 5,000 languages in the world and we can't find one that we both understand." In anger, the wife replied, "What in the world are you talking about?" The cartoon was intended to be humorous, but how true to life! In addition to words, there are countless ways in which we communicate.

Our language contains some powerful expressions that can often produce magical fruits. They are: "I love you," "thank you," and "I'm sorry." When said with sincerity, these expressions convey love, appreciation and willingness to compromise and resolve conflicts. Some find it most difficult to say "I'm sorry," especially when they are convinced they are right. Saying "I'm sorry" should be accompanied with some gentle, nonverbal body language—holding a spouse's hand, looking into another's eyes, responding with a loving hug.

There are other ways to say "I'm sorry" which will pave the way to restore harmony. When it is hard to ask for forgiveness or say "I'm sorry," a written note strategically placed can offer an apology. A note will give the partner some time to reconsider and enable him or her to more easily forgive.

Card shops offer greeting cards for every occasion, including messages to calm marital crises. If it is not a major disagreement, a card can adequately express our sentiments. In fact, card shops are equipped to print our own personal message within a few minutes while we wait. We can even record our own voice expressing our sentiment on a "talking card." A card can pave the way for a peaceful settlement of a family difficulty. It is a healing balm.

A familiar advertisement reminds us of the magic of flowers. Florists have capitalized on the slogan, "Say it with flowers."™ Flowers symbolize love, care, concern, and appreciation. Their beauty has an inherent touch of magic.

Paul and Marie were celebrating their twentieth wedding anniversary with a leisurely breakfast with their family when a bouquet of long-stemmed red roses arrived. Their eight-year-old daughter Mary Ann looked at the roses and gasped, "A dollar fifty apiece!" When her father asked how she knew this, his daughter replied, "I went to the store yesterday to buy a rose for mother, but I just had seventy-two cents." Marie was a resourceful mother. She hugged her daughter, reassuring Mary Ann that she herself was the most precious rose she'd ever received.

ENRICHMENT

When a couple feels that there is "something missing" in their relationship, it is often because they lack honest sharing with each other or take the other person too much for granted. A simple, four-step program outlining a method of communication can greatly enrich their lives together.

Husband and wife can initiate the program by first resolving to spend some time together regularly in an unhurried, relaxed sharing of their thoughts and feelings about themselves, about each other and about the happenings in their lives. Generously giving our time is truly a gift of self.

As a couple moves into the second step, a genuine spirit of appreciation and affection should prevail in their relationship. No one wearies of hearing expressions of love and gratitude from his or her spouse. These expressions manifest a loving concern for each other and solidify the marital union.

Love and laughter should characterize the third step in the process of building good communications. Laughter is an indication of seeing the silver lining in every cloud appearing on the horizon and also a sign of positive thinking in facing all the eventualities of life.

In a happy, harmonious marriage there must be room for God as the third party of a husband's and wife's mutual contract. Spending time praying together daily will enable husband and wife to be constantly aware of the loving presence of the Lord in their household. Praying together is a powerful matrix in marriage, for the Lord is the source of the love, peace, and joy we all desire.

DIVINE WELLSPRING

Husbands and wives who maintain a deep personal relationship with the Lord and strive to cooperate with his grace will surely be able to preserve real peace and harmony, mutual understanding, and cooperation in their married life. Married couples would do well to reflect often that marriage is a way of life instituted by the Lord himself. They should always be mindful that the Lord planned from all eternity that they should meet, fall in love, and commit their lives to this sublime vocation for life.

Marriage is a sacrament instituted by Jesus as a means for a couple to grow in holiness, to help sanctify each other, and eventually attain their eternal salvation. God shares his divine love with them that they may love each other and that their love might increase and mature throughout the years. The Lord generously supplies them with the continual grace they need to welcome and educate their children.

With the Lord's abiding presence and his promised assistance, couples will be enabled to resist the onslaughts threatening the institution of marriage. Married couples need the special grace of the sacrament to offset the widespread disregard for the sacredness of marriage in today's society. With the influences of evil so rampant, a marital union can easily be threatened by discord, by a spirit of domination, infidelity, jealousy, and other conflicts that can lead to hatred and separation. To offset these threats to their marital union, husbands and wives need the help of God's grace which he will never deny to anyone who humbly implores him. The Lord said to Paul and to us, "My grace is sufficient for you, for power is made perfect in weakness" (2 Cor 12:9).

WITH YOU ALWAYS

The teachings of the Church assure us of the enduring presence and power of the Lord with us at all times.

"Christ dwells with them (married couples), gives them the strength to take up their crosses and so follow him, to rise again after they have fallen, to forgive one another, to bear one another's burdens, to be 'subject to one another out of reverence for Christ,' and to love one another with a supernatural, tender and fruitful love. In the joys of their love and family life he gives them here on earth a foretaste of the wedding feast of the Lamb" (*Catechism of the Catholic Church*, par. 1642).

Jesus promised that he would never leave us orphans, but would be with us always. He is present in every home as he was in the home at Nazareth, thus making every home a domestic church. He also told us, "Without me you can do nothing" (Jn 15:5), which is another way of saying that with him we can do all he asks of us.

At the wedding feast in Cana (Jn 2) Jesus celebrated the sacredness of marriage. He proved his loving concern for the married couple and the guests by responding to the intercession of his Mother when she informed him that the wine was running out. With the cooperation of the servers, Jesus was able to work his first miracle. When he asked the servers to fill the six stone jars with water, they did so even though it was a difficult task to carry the water from a spring some distance away.

Mary is equally concerned about us and the welfare of our family. As she said to the servers, "Do whatever he tells you," she is advising married couples to do the same. When husband and wife are receptive to the Lord's directives, he will change the water of mediocrity in their lives into the sparkling wine of love, peace, and joy.

Prayer

Loving Father, you have blessed and sustained us in the bond of marriage. Please continue to increase our love throughout the joys and sorrows of life. We ask this through Christ, our Lord. Amen

NINE

———⇒▶◀⇐———

Trauma of Moving

Our society has rapidly become a mobile, itinerant people. The old family home with its traditions, memories, and lore is fading into oblivion, no longer being handed down from one generation to another. Many reasons contribute to the mobility of our times. Business and employment often require moving to a different location. Families in the military are frequently reassigned. Comfortable and rapid means of transportation have wooed many away from their place of birth.

Even though the abode we call home is not as permanent as in former times, home can still be a haven of peace and protection, an escape from the noise, speed, and confusion of the world beyond its walls. At home we bask in love, loyalty, security, and sensitivity found nowhere else in the world.

ON THE MOVE

William, his devoted wife, Barbara, and their three children deeply appreciated their comfortable, conveniently located home in the city they loved. One evening when William arrived

89

home from his office, it was apparent that something was troubling him; he ate little at dinner; he was not his customary light-hearted conversationalist and did not seem interested in the children's activities of the day, as was his wont. He had earlier called Barbara to break the news that he was asked to become the CEO of a larger branch of the company in another city. While this promotion was welcome with its increase in salary to help finance the children's college education, it was also devastating, since it necessitated leaving the home they loved and moving to another city. When he announced the news over the phone to his wife, her immediate response was a cheerful congratulations. But then the realization of uprooting their family, moving to a strange location and giving up their beautiful home brought tears to her eyes as she spoke. "We will talk about it later this evening. I will let you explain it to the children."

Over dessert that evening, William told the children what was going to happen soon in their family. His announcement was greeted with an outcry of disappointment and anguish. Each of the children voiced a different reason for not wanting to move, leave their friends and go to a strange school. While he was gently struggling with the children's objections, he noticed tears in Barbara's eyes as she stealthily wiped them away.

Sleep did not come easily to William that night. As he tossed and turned in bed, the objections and disappointments of the children re-echoed in his mind. "Dad, I'm a junior and will probably be on the varsity football team next year. In another school, I would have to begin all over again," was Bob's first objection. "Besides I've been working hard hoping to get a scholarship next year. Maybe I could stay here and live with one of my friends." Next in his mind he replayed Nancy's feelings as a freshman in high school. "Daddy, when I started high school, it took me a long time to make new friends and I don't want to leave them. It would be so hard to begin again." Their darling Libby, age ten, asked, "If we have to move, could I bring Susie with me, because she is my special playmate and I know she would never want me to leave her." (Susie, a nine-year old spastic child, lived next door.) William welcomed the morning and with bleary eyes went off to work.

The next evening at dinner, the children were still asking why and registering objections against moving so far away. William then informed them of his plan for the family. In two weeks they would have their spring break from school. He was going to take the week off and, as a family, they would travel to the city they would soon call home. He also told them that they would be looking at some houses, and they would have to help their mother and him to make a decision on which one they liked best. They would also look into the neighborhood and the school situation. Would they agree to this plan? In the meantime, his office was exploring the housing market to discover a few suitable homesites.

In the quiet of their bedroom, Barbara told him how much she admired his handling this traumatic situation so masterfully. She said, "I know how much you are hurting and how you loathe to move away from all your friends, yet you showed loving concern and consideration for me and the children." Only then did William permit his own feelings to show.

PAINFUL DETACHMENTS

William found it painful to leave his elderly mother who needed extra help occasionally. Even though she was in good hands and well taken care of, he would miss his regular visits with her. His deep love for her made the parting painful.

Moving has some advantages, often giving us an opportunity to get rid of some unused and unneeded objects. In the process of getting ready to move, William discovered that he had become unduly attached to many of the things accumulated over the years, making it very hard to give them up.

As a faithful churchgoer he had served on different committees and made close friends whom he would greatly miss. Recently, he had been elected chairman of his service club. Resigning his post and parting from many dear friends would leave a void in his life. Breaking up a long-standing golf foursome would cause sadness for all four.

Leaving faithful co-workers would not be easy. He saw tears in several eyes when news of his departure was announced. Nor was packing, transporting, unpacking, and setting up anew a happy prospect. With all this pain in leaving, he hoped the family trip to the new city would help them begin the adjustment process.

EXPLORATORY EXPEDITION

As agreed, two weeks later the whole family was inspecting three different houses in the city to which they would soon be moving. Each one had a pad and pencil to jot down features they thought were important in each house, as well as the disadvantages they saw. It was a long day with hours of minute inspections and dozens of questions posed to the realtor.

Afterwards, the family loaded up with hamburgers and beverages and went to a nearby park for the evening meal and a decision-making session. Each person was to point out the features they considered important in each one of the three houses they inspected and then cast their vote for the house they considered best suited for their needs. The houses were listed #1, #2 and #3, in the order in which they were visited. The discussion was long and detailed, but was not without a few lighter comments made by the children. Bob liked house #3 and had already chosen the room which would be his bedroom. Nancy liked the family room in #3 so that she could entertain her new friends when she found some. Libby was impressed with the large backyard and lawn in #3 because she might be able to get a pony and corral it there. Mother and dad had more practical reasons, but also favored house #3. As

Bob had hoped, the trip was a strategic step in helping the family make the transition less painful.

DREAM HOME

Betty was a single parent, a mother of three children: Peter 14, Doug 12, and Mary 9. When her husband was killed in a plane crash she was left alone to care for the family. She taught and wrote to support her family, but barely made ends meet with nothing laid aside for her children's future education. She lived in a modest house which she and her late husband had transformed into a comfortable, beautiful dwelling for themselves and their three children. She enjoyed her home and treasured its happy memories. When the accident claimed the life of her husband, everything changed. Her financial worries were many. Friends and neighbors were always helpful, but the heartache was painful.

Unexpectedly, she was offered a lucrative teaching position at a university in a distant city. Her first thought was, "How could I give up my dream home?" Accepting this position would require selling her home and moving away from friends and relatives. She felt her heart would break every time she thought of giving up her home, but she desperately needed the additional income to support her family. Heartbreaking as it seemed, the decision was obvious. The Lord permits pain to prepare us for greater gifts.

For nearly forty years John and Anne had called 37 Pine Street their home. The years had flown by and their children were all settled in their own homes. The years had taken their toll on both of them. John could no longer mow the lawn or keep up their garden plot. Even though many of the rooms of their home were empty, Anne found keeping up the house too exhausting. A decision was inevitable, even though the very thought of it was heartrending.

They bought a spacious apartment in a retirement complex

with a magnificent view of the countryside. The very thought of leaving their home with its countless memories was traumatic. Disposing of the myriad of things they had accumulated over the years required a great spirit of detachment. As they were getting settled in their new living quarters, John summed it up, "The Lord has given and the Lord has taken away, but we bless the Lord because we still have each other."

PAINFUL GOODBYES

Farewells and separations, even though temporary, are part of the pangs of life. A sanctuary banner message reminds us, "Earth is a continual goodbye; heaven is an eternal hello." Young men and women leaving home to pursue their college education or enlisting for military service will experience the pains of loneliness and homesickness. Paradoxically, this pain can produce good fruits, engendering a deeper love and appreciation of the family and home they left. Similarly, the joys of newly married couples are punctuated with nostalgic feelings as they separate from family and friends. Missionaries, volunteers, businessmen, and employees assigned overseas not only endure loneliness and homesickness, but also find cultural adjustments difficult and painful. How good to know that not a single heartache is in vain!

SPIRITUAL COMFORT

To soothe some of the heartache when we are asked to move our home to another location, recall that God loves each one of us so very much that he would never permit any suffering or hardship to afflict us, unless he could bring some good out of it. Every sorrow and disappointment conditions us for a further maturing in our relationship with the Lord, and leads us into a deeper dependence upon him. Suffering also helps us understand that when his will conflicts with ours, he will enlighten and strengthen us to recognize our self-centeredness and our limited horizon. Many of us have experienced failure, frustration, suffering, and disappointment when we were burdened with some hardship which seemed unjust, only to discover some time later what a great blessing it was in our life. The hardships involved in moving to another home may be quite traumatic but they will bring untold blessings in their wake if we are open to them.

Nothing happens by chance, for God plans every detail of life for our own spiritual and temporal welfare. When it is necessary to change our residence, be it near or far, different people will cross our path. In God's inscrutable plan, we will have an influence on our new acquaintances and they will also touch us in some way. The Lord radiates his abiding presence in us to others, even without our being aware of it.

When we move from one area to another, there is a specific task awaiting us there, a task no one else in all the world can fulfill. Just as no one can love for us, no one but we ourselves can fulfill the mission to which the Lord calls us. This truth demands our trust in God's providential love, guiding and encouraging us in fulfilling his mysterious plans.

When Marty was transferred by his company to a distant city, he was deeply distressed. Little did he realize what God had in mind for him. Marty was upset and angry since he would have to leave his buddies who were all single and enjoying their life together. In due time God began to reveal his plan to Marty. He met Virginia and sometime later she became his bride. Our God is a God of surprises.

A PATH TO FOLLOW

In sacred Scripture we find a number of inspirational examples to encourage us in our anxiety about moving. First and foremost are the words and example of Jesus, who never asks us to accept anything which he himself does not share with us. We can well appreciate the pain that he, as well as his Mother, experienced when the time arrived for him to leave the peaceful surroundings of Nazareth and move into a hostile world to bring the Good News of salvation to all mankind. His journey from home into his mission field ended in his redemptive death, which brought eternal life to all of us.

In spite of his advanced years, Abraham was asked to leave his kinsfolk and homeland to go to an unknown land which the Lord would show him. In his exile, away from the worship of false gods, Abraham was able to preserve for posterity the belief in the one true God. Since family ties were strong, his farewell to his homeland and his venturing into the unknown must have caused him much pain and anxiety. Today we are reaping the fruits of his sacrifice.

The apostles, including St. Paul, had to leave home to bring the Gospel message to a waiting world. Even though they were motivated by great love for the Lord, they were also very human and must have felt great distress over leaving home and loved ones. We are grateful for all they endured in bringing us the way of life Jesus laid down for us to follow.

Down through the ages men and women have left home and country to serve others in many worthy causes. Although they were motivated by zeal and love for the Lord and their fellowmen, they endured sorrow and pain in departing and separating from family and friends. As their lives attest, the Lord filled them with peace and joy. The Lord continues to bring countless blessings out of the trauma of moving.

Prayer

Father, you remind us that our ways are not your ways, so that we do not lose heart when our will conflicts with your will. Help us always to say "yes" to whatever you may send us and the strength to fulfill your call all the days of our life. Amen

TEN

―――⇒▶●◀⇐―――

Crisis of Alcohol Addiction

In our society it is customary to serve refreshments or snacks when small groups meet for a business session or a social gathering. These goodies enhance the conviviality and enjoyment of the guests, helping them to get better acquainted and to share more freely with those present.

On more formal occasions, at social hours and cocktail parties, alcoholic beverages are served. Enjoying a drink helps us relax, stimulates conversation, and soothes the cares and demands of the day. While these celebrations are happy occasions, some guests may be struggling with an addiction to and a dependency on alcohol, and may drink to excess.

Moderate drinkers are able to control both the frequency and quantity of alcoholic beverages they consume. They can take it or leave it alone. They do not have too much difficulty in giving up drinking entirely if a sufficient reason warrants it, such as ill health, a doctor's advice, encouragement of a spouse or family, or a self-awareness that a desire for alcohol is increasing within them. They may discover that drinking somewhat impairs them physically and mentally. Moderate drinkers usually do not find it too difficult to abstain completely since they are not addicted and their will is sufficiently strong to enable them to persevere in their resolve.

ON THE ROAD

Some people who begin drinking moderately gradually develop a greater desire for the euphoria they experience while drinking. They need alcohol to satisfy real or imaginary needs. They convince themselves that they have to have a drink to quiet their nerves, to relieve tension, to bolster their courage, to prove themselves socially acceptable. Peer pressure urges them not to be a non-drinking oddball. Without realizing it, they travel quite far down the road to becoming helpless, powerless alcoholics.

"REJOICE IN HOPE"

Alcoholism is a deceptive, destructive, puzzling, and powerful addiction that renders a person powerless to overcome the habit. For people who have lost control of their lives, there is hope and promise if they are willing to implore the Lord's healing and cooperate with his grace and the other means available. In his Word the Lord admonishes us, "Rejoice in hope, endure in affliction, persevere in prayer" (Rom 12:12). For some time it was erroneously thought that willpower alone would enable an alcoholic to be cured of this illness. Experience has proven otherwise.

In everything we do in life, we need the Lord's inspiration and assistance. Did he not say, "Without me, you can do nothing" (Jn 15:5)? He is always at our beck and call. We can obtain his guidance and strength by praying fervently and consistently for a physical, emotional, and spiritual healing. The

Lord's help comes to us in what is called grace. Grace is God's gift gratuitously given to anyone who asks for it. In begging him to help us overcome the addiction of alcohol, he assures us as he did Paul, "My grace is sufficient for you, for power is made perfect in weakness" (2 Cor 12:9). God can and does heal instantly and miraculously, but he seldom does so. Rather, he asks us to use all the other means at our disposal to build a solid front against the enemy.

God's grace enables us to use these means and put them into practice in our lives. There is a spiritual program devised to help anyone with a drinking problem called Alcoholics Anonymous. It is God ("Higher Power") oriented, recognizing our powerlessness and our dire need for the Lord's help.

ALCOHOLICS ANONYMOUS

People who have lost control of their lives and are powerless over alcohol need not despair. There is hope and promise in a program called Alcoholics Anonymous. It is not so much an organization, but a voluntary fellowship of men and women from every station in life who have lost control of their lives by their excessive drinking. They meet regularly to learn more about themselves, the cause of their addiction, and their lack of control. They come together to encourage and assist one another on the road to sobriety. There is only one membership requirement—an earnest desire to stop drinking completely. In most populous areas AA meetings are held every day of the week at convenient hours, giving well-intentioned people opportunities to attend. In a moderately sized city, there are an average of over two hundred AA meetings listed each week. These meetings are usually small gatherings with a wonderful spirit of friendliness, mutual concern, and understanding. This program is open to anyone with a drinking or addiction problem. It boasts a phenomenal success record.

THE FIRST STEP

To convince excessive drinkers to begin the AA program is no easy task. Most drinkers maintain that they are not alcoholics and are in control of their own drinking. They are reluctant to admit that they need help and are fearful that their drinking problem will become known among their friends, causing them embarrassment and social and economic damage. Parents, spouses, and friends may find it impossible to convince a problem drinker to seek help in the AA program. A recovering alcoholic who has found sobriety in AA can more easily persuade other alcoholics that they need help. A recovering alcoholic tries to win the confidence of problem drinkers and gradually lead them to recognize that they are powerless over alcohol and that a friendly welcome awaits them at every meeting. Recovering alcoholics volunteer to sponsor problem drinkers in the program.

A well-known clergyman was a popular speaker at conferences and retreats. During the course of a retreat, one of the retreatants approached him explaining that he had a problem. The clergyman invited him to sit down and asked, "What is your problem?" The retreatant replied, "You are my problem. You are an alcoholic and you need help." The clergyman tried to deny it and assured him that he did not need help. Whereupon he said, "Look, I am a recovering alcoholic and you can't fool me."

In due time, he sponsored the clergyman in AA. After his recovery was well underway, he spent all his time, talent, and energy leading retreats and conferences, sometimes called Serenity Workshops, for those who have drinking problems.

The testimony of Father Bill illustrates the pattern of many problem drinkers on their way back to normalcy.

Here are a few thoughts on my passing from darkness into light.

Over the course of some twenty years, alcohol became my support under stress, my escape from myself and my ally in difficult situations. I began to frequent bars and taverns because drinking there helped me to relate more freely with people; loneliness was easier to bear.

As the years went by I began to feel more and more like a hypocrite—a Dr. Jekyll and Mr. Hyde. I was going through the motions of my work; my family relationships became a burden. Alcohol and alcoholic behavior gave me a feeling of happiness and freedom for the moment, but it was always followed by guilt and depression. Eventually, I "hit the bottom" in a psychiatric hospital. Recovery was painful and humiliating. But it was in this emotional, psychological, and spiritual chaos that I began to experience the mercy and goodness of God in a new way.

Now I have been happily in recovery for almost eight years; I am learning to experience true freedom and peace. My depression has gone for the most part, and I am functioning with alacrity and peace of mind. Family and social relationships have been restored to a point of enjoyment. In all of this turmoil, I am learning the truth of what Anthony de Mello, SJ said, "Repentance reaches fullness when you are brought to gratitude for your sins."[1]

A multiplicity of testimonies could be cited to prove the effectiveness of the AA program for anyone prepared to submit to its directives.

The program of Alcoholics Anonymous is not an instantaneous or magical cure-all. It must be faithfully and perseveringly followed for many years or even a lifetime, but the dividends outweigh all the efforts put into it.

AL-ANON

Family members, faced with an alcoholic problem in the home, may be overwhelmed with feelings of shame and resentment. They may become angry, perplexed, and frustrated, not knowing what they can and should do or where to find help. They will find great comfort and direction in a program specially designed for them called the Al-Anon program.

Al-Anon is a program made up of individuals and families striving to cope with the excessive drinking of an associate or loved one. In Al-Anon meetings nondrinking members learn that alcoholism is an illness, an addiction affecting the minds, bodies, and spirits of drinkers. It is an addiction which may cause insanity and lead to earlier death. Al-Anon is designed for mutual sharing and support, thereby helping one another to handle feelings of frustration. This open sharing leads people to a change in their own attitude which is greatly beneficial to themselves and may also help bring the alcoholic into the Twelve-Step recovery program. Al-Anon is entirely separate from the Alcoholics Anonymous program, but it does use the general principles of the AA program as a guide for husbands, wives, relatives, friends, and others associated with an alcoholic.

PROSPECTIVE CANDIDATES

Who should attend these meetings and how can they expect to be helped by coming together regularly? Perhaps the most effective way of presenting the fruits and advantages of the Al-Anon program is to list a few testimonies of individuals, many of whom at first resisted even the thought of attending the meetings, but who have since discovered it to be a real boon in their lives.

Frank was greatly agitated over his twenty-four-year-old son, Bill, whose drinking had carried him well down the road to becoming an alcoholic. Frank tried to reason with him, argued with him, and even threatened to disown him completely, but to no avail. After joining an Al-Anon group, Frank better understood that his own feelings of disgust and anger were harmful to himself and would not help his son. After attending regular meetings, Frank accepted the fact that alcoholism is a disease and needs medical treatment. Through Al-Anon, Frank found a young man about the same age as his son, Bill, who volunteered to confront Bill and to try to lead him into recovery.

Until recent months, Isabel had always been a happy, cheerful person and a delight to be with. Then a great change came over her—she became angry, confused, and depressed most of the time because of the constant drinking of her husband, who often arrived home drunk. She was unable to reason with him. Her pleading fell on deaf ears. She considered herself a total failure in trying to make him realize the damage he was doing to himself and his family. The Al-Anon group was a real godsend to her.

Bernard, a well-known, respected attorney, rarely accepted a social invitation, not knowing if his wife, Mabel, would be sufficiently sober to accompany him. He felt guilty about fabricating excuses to cover up for her drinking. Unfortunately, Bernard maintains that he would be too uncomfortable to seek help by joining an Al-Anon group.

Emily became very disturbed when her family's routine was upset or the family meal delayed because of her husband's drinking with the boys after work. She found it difficult to make excuses to her children. She frequently pleaded with her husband, "If you really love me and the children, you would quit drinking," which seemed to drive him to drink even more to rid himself of guilt feelings. Through Al-Anon Emily discovered that her tactics were ineffective; now she is beginning to cope with herself and her husband's drinking with the hope of a brighter future.

These are a few of the lives that have been changed and enriched by following the Al-Anon program. Al-Anon meetings can be as effective for the nondrinker as AA meetings are for the alcoholic. Many marriages have been saved and peace restored in families. For them, the promise of a brighter future looms on the horizon.

ALATEEN

Alateen is part of the Al-Anon program. While it follows closely the outline of Al-Anon, it is directed primarily to teenage children of alcoholics. Taking part in this program with their peers, who live in the same atmosphere at home, has helped young people, especially when they have found new friends with whom they can share heartaches and disappointments. The anger, shame, and resentment which they harbor are gradually replaced with an acceptance, promising hope and peace in the future.

Brad was an angry, sullen teenager who hated his dad, who was intoxicated most of the time. When his dad was drinking heavily, he often struck Brad, called him vile names, and even cursed him. Many times Brad intended to leave home, but his mother, Margaret, told him that she depended on him to keep her own sanity under the conditions at home. After Margaret was introduced to the Al-Anon program, she persuaded Brad to attend Alateen meetings. Gradually Brad learned about alcohol, especially that it was an illness over which his father was powerless. As he and his mother found some relief in their sharing together, Brad's hatred and anger began to subside.

Faithful attendance at the Alateen meetings and a firm resolve to follow the suggestions offered bring peace of mind and heart to the teen members. In more than one instance, teens have had great influence on their alcoholic parents.

When a recovering alcoholic and his or her family strives to live in a peaceful relationship with the Lord, with themselves, with others and also with creation, they will find hope and encouragement, strength and serenity in handling the problems which face them. The Lord is faithful to his promise: "My peace, I give to you."

Serenity Prayer

God grant me the serenity to accept
the things I cannot change,
courage to change the things I can,
and wisdom to know the difference. Amen

ELEVEN

———◈———

Loss of Employment

L ife on earth may be compared to taking an extensive car trip through a country. On our journey we encounter various kinds of terrain. In some places we can enjoy the vast plains, lush with meadows of green grass for grazing, fertile fields to replenish our food supply. As we continue our travels, we come upon some hilly country decked with trees and other vegetation. These hills are not too difficult to negotiate, but they do caution us to drive with greater care. In another part of the country we gaze upon the imposing mountains with steep precipices plunging into the valleys below. Climbing these makes our driving more hazardous, slowing down our progress somewhat.

Traveling through the countryside reflects our journey down the road of life. When all is going smoothly, and few problems arise, our journey is similar to driving through level country. Life is quite uncluttered and peaceful. The hills of life are the disappointments and hardships that arise from time to time, none of which creates a crisis situation. Usually we can cope with them even though they cause us some inconvenience and struggle. The mountains with the deep valleys encircling their bases are the critical happenings which confront us. They may be major reverses, setbacks, losses, disappointments, trials, and tribulations of any kind, which we experience as we trudge down the pathway of life. Attempting to handle these tragic and traumatic events may seem insurmountable—similar to climbing a steep mountain. However, we must keep climbing or risk being plunged into the deep valley of discouragement, depression, and despair. One mountainous problem that looms up frequently in our time is the loss of gainful employment or other income to support our family.

SHATTERED DREAM

Ken was confronted with such a problem that left him discouraged, disheartened, and uncertain about what the future held in store for him and his family. A few years ago, Ken built a large grocery store in a developing neighborhood. He worked long, hard hours and was scrupulously honest and accommodating to all his customers. His employees were loyal and worked hard to fulfill their duties. Ken's outgoing personality won him many friends. At this time, his journeying was over the level plains of life. Naturally, a few problems arose, like the hills on life's journey, but by compromising and adjusting, solutions were soon found.

After Ken was well established and his business was doing well, a steep craggy mountain, with its gloomy, foreboding peaks loomed up in front of him. A supermarket and a chain drug store were being built in the vicinity of his business. After the grand opening, Ken's business began to dwindle. Heartrending as it was, Ken had to terminate two of his special employees: Joan was a single parent supporting her family on her salary; Ted was working his way through college. Ken could not compete with the big companies, nor could he offer his customers the long hours his competition gave to their patrons.

The handwriting was on the wall and the final outcome

inevitable. Ken was so crushed, embarrassed, and humiliated that he tried to avoid people, which was diametrically different from his natural personality. He worried how he could support his family. His ambition of being a neighborhood merchant was shattered; his hope of helping the needy by employing them was thwarted. The "For Sale" sign on the front door of his dream store was the last straw which severely challenged his faith. His greatest comfort was the unwavering support of his wife who continued to reassure him that God had other plans for him and that he would provide in his own mysterious way.

Ken and his wife often shared the words of Scripture with each other. In this crisis, they found much comfort in the Lord's invitation,

"Come to me, all you who labor and are burdened, and I will give you rest. Take my yoke upon you and learn from me for I am meek and humble of heart; and you will find rest for yourselves. For my yoke is easy, and my burden light."

Matthew 11:28ff

They also found great reassurance in the Lord's promise, "I am with you always, until the end of the age" (Mt 28: 20).

EFFECTS OF JOBLESSNESS

On our journey through life, we encounter various kinds of losses—all of them painful, some even disastrous. High on the list of distressful losses for both men and women is the loss of employment. It may be referred to as laid-off, terminated, fired, or let go—all harsh words with dire consequences.

Losing a job means losing a sense of our personhood. We look upon ourselves as a failure with an inability to earn an income to support ourselves and our family. This can be greatly humiliating since it is often accompanied by a loss of our status in the community and the niche in our social life. For the most part, unemployed people feel that there is a stigma attached to them since they lost the source of livelihood so essential to daily living.

With no guaranteed income, monthly bills may not be paid, insurance may be terminated since premiums cannot be met, and merchandise purchased with time payments may be repossessed. For some families, failure to meet house payments may result in eviction with all its dreadful consequences. A lack of income may necessitate getting rid of some possessions such as a second car, or other objects not crucial to our daily living. If we are severely impoverished, we may have to seek financial help, causing us great embarrassment. In some instances, loss of employment may disrupt the home so completely that it causes a breakup of the family and may even lead to divorce. Ultimately, lack of income may drive some persons into the world of homelessness.

DEPRESSION

Being severed from the work force may plunge a person into a state of clinical depression. Many depressed persons think that a change of environment may help them escape from depression without realizing that this malady will follow them. If we observe the eyes of the person suffering depression, we can detect the sadness, the hopelessness, the discouragement lingering there. Depression may even create suicidal tendencies within certain people. These are but a few of the horrible effects that a loss of employment can bring into our life. In order to surmount these losses and survive, we must develop a strong faith and trust in the Lord's providential care.

SUDDEN TERMINATION

Pat worked for a certain construction firm for twenty-three years. As a foreman, he supervised various building projects and was regarded as an intelligent, hardworking boss by those with whom he worked. Without any forewarning J.B., the owner, called him into his office to inform him that while they were satisfied and happy with his performance over the years, they were being forced to terminate his employment. The owner alleged two reasons for this decision. J.B.'s son had finished his college course and would take over Pat's position. After further discussion, he admitted that Pat had received several pay increases and that they could no longer afford to pay him the amount he had rightly accumulated over the years. He also maintained that in the business world today it is a common practice to release longtime employees who have reached a high point on the wage scale in order to hire those employees at the bottom of the pay scale.

As usually happens to a person who has suffered a grave loss, Pat experienced some personal reactions with varying lengths of time intervening between each stage.

1. **Disbelief.** Pat left the office dazed; he could not believe what he had just heard—he was laid off permanently. He was out of a job.

2. **Anger.** As he pondered the conversation with his boss, his anger blazed up: How could he do this to me? Where is his sense of justice and concern?

3. **Bargaining.** He was tempted to discuss the matter with J.B. with the hope that some other arrangements could be devised. After some thought he gave up the idea.

4. **Depression.** Pat found himself getting very depressed. His reputation in the construction business was at stake. With two sons in college, he needed every cent he could earn. How could he face his friends?

5. **Acceptance.** As the months rolled by, Pat moved into the fifth stage realizing that what had happened was over. He had to accept his lot and get on with his life.

After his being dismissed from his company, some very positive changes began to happen in Pat's life. His wife suggested that he might want to help an elderly, widowed neighbor whose home needed some repairs. Pat responded and, with the other volunteers, they refurbished and repainted the little cottage, making it into a real dream home. Other requests from the neighborhood, and far beyond, began to come in until Pat found himself back in business, this time for himself. Today, Pat has a small but successful construction business of his own.

HUMANE TRANSITION

In some companies such transitions can be made with less pain and confusion. Don owned a successful advertising agency for many years. The time of retirement caught up with him. At a staff meeting he explained that he was looking forward to retirement and had a few suggestions on where they might find new jobs when he closed the agency. He had already been in contact with other agencies who would be willing to hire some of them, provided they wished to join the staff. His employees were gratified at his humane understanding and his concern in trying to find other employment for them.

Don had a second suggestion to present to them: if they were so inclined, he would be willing to sell his own advertising agency to the staff for a nominal price. They could make an annual payment to supplement his retirement benefits. He intended to retire in about six months, giving them some time to consider either one of these options, or to take any other course they wished.

The staff made their decision and in a few months an agreement was reached and signed: they would continue the agency as employee-owned, retaining Don's name as it was known throughout the years. After that was settled, he made one more statement to be added to the agreement. Since his wife had preceded him in death and they had no children, in the event of his death, the agency would belong to the employees, free and clear. This was Don's way of expressing his gratitude for their hard work and loyalty throughout the years.

SCALING THE MOUNTAIN

Monday mornings were an especially difficult time for George. Plagued with a drinking problem, he usually indulged too freely over the weekends and had to drag himself off to work with a severe hangover. The quality of his work suffered; his fellow employees were not sympathetic, but rather critical of his behavior.

His supervisor warned him many times about his excessive drinking, noting that it was to blame for the unsatisfactory quality of his work. Eventually George was fired. Since it was not the first job he had lost because of his addiction, he was burdened with tremendous guilt feelings and dreaded facing his wife and children. He was ashamed to face his friends and former fellow employees.

As expected, his wife and children were greatly disturbed and disappointed once again. Too often he had broken his promise to quit drinking, only to fall again. Once more his wife was frustrated and disillusioned. Without her salary, the family would not survive. With feelings of guilt and failure overwhelming him, George drank even more to escape into the oblivion he found in alcohol.

In this sad state of affairs the Lord sent a Good Samaritan in the person of a fellow employee who arrived at his door to inform George that he was taking him to an AA meeting that evening. That was nearly a year ago and George and his recovering sponsor have not missed a single weekly meeting since. With God's grace, the support of his family and the help of the AA program, George is on the way to recovery.

LESSONS IN CARELESSNESS

Gerry was hired by an employee-owned grocery store with the assurance that he could eventually share in the ownership if he proved himself. He was always full of life and had a good sense of humor. He was a carefree type of person who was not too dependable. The customers enjoyed his wit, but did not come to him with any serious questions.

Frequently he arrived late for work and when it was his turn to unlock the doors, he often kept the early customers waiting outside. Occasionally he would take a day off, offering a flimsy excuse or simply not appearing for work. When the other employees complained, the manager had no choice but to fire Gerry to maintain the morale and spirit of their business venture.

Gerry was shocked when he was fired and could not believe that they could be so cruel; he was angry. He asked for another chance which was not granted. He was deeply depressed and worried about how he was to support his wife and two young children. He was humiliated, ashamed to admit another failure; he could not face his peers.

His wife was disappointed and angry since this was the third job that he had lost because of his lack of responsibility. Her patience was exhausted. She assured him that she loved him, but from now on it was going to be "tough love." After he promised to seek counseling, she informed him that she was going to visit her parents for a month to give him a chance to take an inventory of himself and decide what he was going to do about his irresponsible ways. This was a mortal blow to his ego and in the loneliness of their home after his family left, he had time to think and, ultimately, to change.

SURVIVAL INSIGHTS

The trauma of unemployment leaves us with strong feelings of hopelessness. Whether or not the job loss results from circumstances beyond our control, it plunges us into a devastating sense of helplessness. When it is not within our power to change these factors, we become angry and frustrated. In our pain we lash out at all the people or circumstances that created the trauma in which we find ourselves. Our anger is not only directed at those responsible for our unemployment, but often toward those closest to us.

In order to overcome this emotional upset we need a healing from the anger and frustration besetting us. The Lord is our healer and he is anxious and eager to heal us if we are open to his healing power. We can turn to him with a brief prayer, "Lord, heal me," to be repeated quietly many times until the anger is calmed. It may be necessary to repeat this prayer throughout the day each time anger wells up again.

HOPELESSNESS

When hopelessness arises within us, we can see nothing but futility in even trying to better our situation. Our moods change from time to time and may drag us down into a state of depression. To rid ourselves of this sense of despair, we need to remind ourselves that the Lord loves us with a providential love and will never permit anything to happen to us from which he cannot bring some good for us. If we lose our job, be assured that he has another mission for us in some area, perhaps as yet unknown to us. He personally gave us this reassurance when he said, "For I know well the plans I have in mind for you, says the Lord, plans for your welfare, not for woe! Plans to give you a future full of hope. When you call me, when you go to pray to me, I will listen to you. When you look for me, you will find me with you" (Jer 29:11ff).

Prayer

In Scripture, the necessity of having a firm hope is mentioned repeatedly to encourage us never to lose hope, regardless of how gloomy our life may seem. For a closing prayer, we suggest that you take some quiet time to reflect on the Lord's Word to us in the following passage from Scripture.

"Affliction produces endurance, and endurance proven character, and proven character, hope, and hope does not disappoint, because the love of God has been poured out into our hearts by the Holy Spirit that has been given to us." **Romans 5:3ff**

TWELVE

Wanderers in the Mist

Some time ago I offered Mass in a mission Church for about one hundred worshippers. As I left the altar at the end of Mass a husband and wife, Dick and Rita, followed me into the sacristy. They were faced with a dilemma and were searching for some guidance for themselves and for their three sons. Mike, their first-born son, aged twenty-four, was married and had one unbaptized child. Mike's wife was a lovely person, a good wife and mother, but had no church affiliations. Mike started missing Mass on Sundays and gradually drifted away from the Church.

Their second son, Roy, was attending college. During his freshman year, he was ridiculed constantly by his peers for going to the Newman Center for Mass. Under such pressure he became rather delinquent and sporadic in receiving the sacraments. Now he claims to have lost his faith altogether and sees no need to practice any religion.

Edward, their youngest son, is in junior high. He still takes his turn at serving Mass and does not seem to have any problem in following his Catholic way of life. However, Dick and Rita are deeply concerned about the influence his older brothers might have on him in the next few years.

Dick and Rita were asking for direction on how they should react toward their two older sons. Should they condemn or condone? Should they invite them to their home? Should they visit them?

I assured them that there were no simple solutions to their problem which has also invaded so many other homes. I promised to stay in touch with them so that together we might gradually discover some steps to take. As we met together in the months to follow, it was evident that Dick and Rita were moving through various phases common to most people who have experienced a grave loss.

At first, these good parents, like so many others, found it difficult to believe that their children were drifting away from the Lord and the way of life they had learned in their home and in their training in school. Was it merely a whim that would pass quickly? I tried to assure them that this defection from the Church was by no means confined to a few families, but is a problem invading countless homes. It is being caused in part by a widespread crisis in faith sweeping our country. Many sons and daughters, as well as other loved ones, are succumbing to the peer pressure of our secularistic society and are wandering in the mist of confusion, uncertainty, doubt and rebellion. Obviously, Dick and Rita were in the first phase of denial.

Some time later, as their disappointment penetrated more deeply, they became angry. After all, they had sacrificed for their children to be educated in their faith, and had tried to set an example in their home. How could their sons dismiss their training so easily without any apparent qualms of conscience? Dick and Rita were surprised that I did not chide them for their occasional outbursts of anger. They were even more surprised when I told them that they were reacting as people normally do when they suffer a great loss.

Some time later when we got together they told me they had decided to pray the rosary together every day, begging God to touch the hearts of their wayward sons and draw them back into the fold. They were bargaining with God and were certain that he would not turn a deaf ear to their prayers. I encouraged them to persevere in praying fervently. I reminded them that asking Mary's intercession through the rosary was an ideal practice. In a totally different context, Mary suffered the pain of loss when Jesus left Nazareth to begin his public ministry. I also cautioned them that their prayers were not in vain, even though God's timetable may not correspond to the one they had set.

The next time I had occasion to meet with Dick and Rita, gloom was written over their faces and their hearts were heavy. In spite of their prayers, they could not detect any change of attitude in their sons who seemed to be wandering even further away from the Lord. Dick and Rita considered themselves utter failures in trying to rear their children. Where had they failed? What did they neglect to do during the past years which would have prevented this crisis? What would their relatives and friends think of their parenting?

They were both overwhelmed with guilt feelings as they recalled some isolated incidents in the years gone by when they reacted in a less than edifying manner that might have shocked their children. Did they become too angry with their children during those turbulent teen years? Dick remembered an occasion when he was upset and extremely angry with his boss and the conditions at his place of work. He voiced his criticism and anger vociferously in front of his children. Did this outburst weaken the faith of his sons?

Before they could recite other similar occasions, I tried to assure them that these guilt feelings were unwarranted since they were not the cause of the loss of faith in their children. I encouraged them to try to throw off these guilt feelings and the gnawing pain of depression by recalling the many happy events which the family enjoyed together. Reliving these wonderful times would counteract these negative feelings as they were remembering the many good years together.

I complimented them for the deep concern and love they had for their sons. I assured them that while their love for their offspring was intense, it was only a shadow of the boundless love the Lord has for their boys. They could be certain that the Lord had his arms around both of them, and young Edward too, and that in the Lord's own time and in his own inscrutable way, he would touch their older boys with a deeper insight into his divine love, causing them to reassess the way of life they were now leading. I encouraged them to read the account of the Parable of the Lost Son (Lk 15:11-32) remembering that the father in this episode is our loving Father in heaven.

After several months I visited Dick and Rita once again. Their whole attitude had changed—the disbelief and anger had passed. They were still bargaining with God, but the depression and discouragement were lifted. They found comfort in praying their daily rosary for their sons. They were elated over the dedication of their youngest son, Edward, who seemed to be a staunch Christian with no evidence of any pernicious influence of his elder brothers. In fact, he was very critical of his brothers' attitude. Dick admitted that this disappointment and loss brought him and Rita closer together and also brought them both into a deeper relationship with the Lord, which was certainly a hidden plus in the Lord's mysterious plan for them.

Dick and Rita experienced a variety of emotions as they passed from one stage to another, which is common for those who are suffering from a great loss. These parents, like so many others, went from the stage of denial, convinced that it could not be happening to them, then to a state of anger and disappointment, and on to bargaining with the Lord followed by depression, and finally an acceptance of loss and a resolve to get on with their lives.

The agonizing pain and frustration which Dick and Rita suffered over the straying of their sons is by no means restricted to their household. The pain of loss, under various guises, is becoming more widespread, almost reaching epidemic proportions. Many families are facing this problem.

The hearts of parents are heavily burdened with worry and disappointment when their children give up the practice of their faith. Parents sometimes experience feelings of guilt, wondering what they neglected to do in training their children. We must understand that we live in an age permeated with a crisis in faith. Young people can easily succumb to the lure of materialism, peer pressure and the sophistication of our times. We must never lose hope for God has his arms around our young people, his desire for their salvation is infinitely greater than ours could ever be. Fervent and persevering prayer for our straying young people will also lighten the burden of anxiety.

- Frank and Jane are the parents of four children, ages six to fourteen. Frank does not attend Mass because he claims he doesn't get anything out of it. He maintains that the homilies are boring, people are unfriendly, the music and singing are not to his liking—and a host of other excuses. Jane is deeply concerned about bringing up her children with a dynamic, operative faith, but does not know how to explain to them why Daddy does not go to Mass with the rest of the family. She is searching for a solution.

- Tony just passed his twenty-first birthday and is heavily into drugs and alcohol. He no longer needs the Lord or the Church. His parents want to know what steps they should take to cope with this situation. What are their obligations to him? He refuses to look for work to support himself.

- A priest friend of mine is not only concerned about the members of his flock who have turned their backs on the sacramental life of the Church, but he is deeply concerned about some members of his immediate family. Of his twenty-four nieces and nephews, only ten are devout Catholics who faithfully practice their religion, one has joined another church, and the rest remain indifferent. He found a little consolation in the fact that only one of his nieces and nephews is divorced.

There is little need to amplify this list. We are all aware of similar cases, since this straying is so rampant in our times. Parents, spouses, and other concerned people are deeply grieved by this crisis in faith which has become a virus in our family life. The discouragement, the pain, and the perplexities have caused many sleepless nights and wearisome days. There is little comfort and consolation since the good people do not know what they can or should do. They feel so helpless.

DO'S AND DON'T'S

What can or should parents and other loved ones do when confronted with the problem of someone straying in the mist away from the Lord?

1. We must realize that the crisis in faith has been caused by many contributing factors. One of the principal causes is the lack of correct information about the Church and her teachings. Many people do not understand that we are living in an age of transition. Others are aware of the transition, but have not been able to adjust to the changing attitude in our relationship with the Lord. At the present time we are in the process of refocusing our motivation in serving the Lord, moving away from a sense of obligation in order to avoid punishment and toward a motivation of love. Genuine love of God will move us into a desire and a longing to do everything to please our loving Father, rather than merely to obey out of a sense of duty.

Only God can judge the human heart. We may not sit in judgment of those wandering in the mist. It is conceivable that these wanderers have rationalized to such an extent that they feel justified in divorcing themselves from the sacramental life of the Church.

Some people who have left the Church have returned after having experienced the Lord's presence and love drawing them into a more personal relationship with him. Others, and this includes those who have left the Church, are struggling since they have not yet had an experiential awareness of the Lord's loving presence in their lives, or have not let themselves be open and receptive to the Lord's love for them.

2. Do not permit a sense of guilt to overwhelm you. Usually those loved ones are sufficiently mature to assume responsibility for their own decisions.

We must remember that rationalization is an insidious enemy and has taken a great toll by weaning many away from the Lord and his Church. Many of those who have strayed have rationalized with themselves to such an extent that they are convinced that they have no need to go to Church or receive the sacraments. They have decided that they can worship God in their own way by taking care of their family, being kind and gracious to others, and helping the poor. One "wanderer" put it in these words, "I have established a profitable and successful business without going to Church. Why should I start now?" Another one said, "I believe in God, but I don't believe in all the ritual and ceremony in the Church." So go the rationalizations. While we may not be able to comprehend their reasoning, we cannot judge them. God alone is the judge.

If we feel that we have made mistakes in rearing our children, there is no need to castigate ourselves. We must keep ourselves aware that the good Lord's grace and influence outweigh our shortcomings. Even if we have seemingly or actually neglected our responsibilities in the past, we ought to humbly ask the Lord's forgiveness and be assured that we are not only forgiven, but that the Lord will intervene in our children's lives and not permit our neglect to lead them astray.

3. Do not nag or preach to your children as they begin to assert their youthful independence. If you do, you may drive a deeper wedge in your relationship with them, even further away from you and your way of life. Some day they may hesitate to come to you when they need you.

Do not try to persuade them to "go to church," but rather try to lead them into a deeper understanding of the Lord as a God who loves them immensely. The Lord himself will draw them to himself in due time. The Lord's love for them is absolutely infinite. He always has his arms around them waiting for them to open their hearts to his love.

4. Pray for them daily, begging the Lord to heal them of any false notion they may have and also to remove whatever barriers are keeping them away from him. There is a simple prayer which you can say countless times throughout the day, "Lord, heal (name)." This is a powerful prayer for healing. You can also use the same prayer for yourself when you feel distraught, worried, or anxious about your loved one who seems to be straying, "Lord, heal me."

If it is feasible, you may be able to encourage your sons or daughters to spend a few moments with the Lord each day in quiet reflection. Urge them to listen with their hearts to what the Lord may be saying to them. Praying in this way may be more appealing to them than the rote prayers they learned as children.

5. Never give up hope. Hope makes us realize that our loved ones, about whom we are deeply concerned, have received the gift of faith as a tiny seed. That seed may seem dormant at this time, but when nurtured by the sunshine of God's grace and love, it could suddenly enlighten and motivate them to recommit their lives to the Lord and walk in his way of life. Hope makes us confident that God will take care of all our day-to-day needs and will never abandon us, not even for an instant. Hope keeps alive within us the realization that God is a loving Father who desires every person be saved and enjoy eternal happiness with him in heaven.

Even though we place our trust and confidence in so good a God, doubts and fears may arise. To avoid becoming discouraged or bitter, hope will keep us mindful that God will always enable us to bring good out of suffering, disappointment, and pain. In this domestic crisis we need a joyful trust in God. "Cast all your worries upon him, because he cares for you" (1 Pt 5:17).

Praying with an expectant faith and a confident hope for a dynamic, enduring trust in God will bring us that peace and consolation the world cannot give.

Prayer

God of mercy, comfort of those in sorrow, the tears of St. Monica moved you to convert her son St. Augustine to the faith of Christ. By their prayers help our loved ones to return to you, to serve you faithfully, and to enjoy the love and peace which you desire for them. Amen

THIRTEEN

Empty-Nest Syndrome

Have all your children left hearth and home to venture out into the world? Do you sigh with relief that they are no longer underfoot, or is there a tug at your heart and an occasional tear in your eye? Little doubt, the latter is closer to the truth.

There comes a time in life when parents may experience an empty-nest syndrome. Time relentlessly marches on. All too soon sons and daughters leave home to begin a new life beyond the confines of the parental abode. Most marry to establish a new home of their own and to rear a family. Business and employment take others miles away. Pursuing a college education accounts for others leaving an empty bed in the "children's room."

Some sons and daughters leave the family nest for less commendable reasons. Some fledglings want to exert their own independence. They no longer want to be restricted by the routine and demands the parental household seems to impose on them, such as regular time for meals, assisting with household chores, and other reasons. The prospect of living in an apartment lures them away from the family residence. Even more painful for parents is when the adult child leaves home to cohabit with a girlfriend or boyfriend, which, unfortunately, is now a trend. This brings great disappointment and anguish to parents whose hearts are already heavily burdened with the exodus of those they love. Drugs and alcohol have lured all too many away from their protected parental environment. Parents are devastated when a son or daughter leaves home to join so-called friends on the street. Departing for this reason injects a piercing thorn into the empty-nest situation. Mothers and fathers cannot help but feel a loneliness, sadness, and heartache at the empty chair at the table or the unslept-in bed in the children's room.

Ann, the mother of four children, said to her friends, "Thank God all my children are on their own and our house is once again peaceful and quiet." Her husband, Dick, added, "Now we are free to travel and do the many things we always wanted to do." Such comments may be honest in some instances, but more often they are an outcry from a lonely heart. Hidden beneath these expressions of euphoria lurk feelings of nostalgia for the constant laughter, the daily hubbub, the endless jingling of the phone, the thunderous music vibrating the walls, and the continuous traffic of friends coming and going.

YOU ARE NOT ALONE

If your empty house causes you heartache, you are in good company. In spirit, visit with Mary the Mother of Jesus and our Mother. Try to imagine the heartache, the loneliness, the emptiness Mary experienced when the time came for Jesus to leave the peaceful solitude of that little home in Nazareth to begin his public ministry. In all probability Joseph was dead, since the Gospel makes no mention of him. This added to

Mary's aloneness. Mary understood very well that the comforting and joyful companionship of Jesus was gone. Furthermore, she was well-versed in the prophecies concerning the Messiah. She knew that Jesus would never return to live in her home in Nazareth. Even more, Mary was painfully aware of the terrible fate which awaited her Son at the hands of his enemies. Jesus' leave-taking of his Mother was so sacred an occasion that the Gospel writers did not enter into the privacy of that event to give us an account of it. Mark alone refers obliquely to this sad parting, "It happened in those days that Jesus came from Nazareth of Galilee and was baptized in the Jordan by John" (Mk 1:9).

When your home seems empty and deserted, pause to reflect that you are not alone. The Lord is living with you and within you. Tell him of your heartache as you ask him to keep your children safe and at peace with him. Your watchword should always be, "Let go and let God." Thank God frequently for the gift of your sons and daughters as you recall the wonderful memories you have of their growing-up years.

DIVERSE REACTIONS

With no two personalities alike, it is naturally expected that parents will react in various ways when confronted with an empty nest. Some will find the adjustment rather difficult, while others will flow with the tide of the events. Perhaps a brief reflection on some instances will enlighten our own situation.

Dan grew up as an only son with three sisters. When Dan married, his mother wept copious tears. These were not the customary tears of joy and excitement usually evident at a beautiful wedding. His mother's tears flowed from a heart deeply hurt at the loss of her only son.

When Dan and his beautiful bride, Beatrice, returned from their honeymoon, his mother has called him every single day without fail. She would inquire about his health, whether or not he was eating properly, was Beatrice a good cook, etc. She repeatedly bemoaned the fact that he did not come to visit her very often. It was quite obvious that Dan's mother had never really let go of her son. She was still clamoring for more of his attention. Dan tried to discourage his mother from checking on him so frequently, but to no avail.

When Dan's mother complained to a friend how deeply hurt she was over the loss of her son, her friend summoned up enough courage to point out that she was making life miserable for the young married couple and also for herself. She tried to explain, as a true friend, that Dan and Beatrice needed time and space to adjust to a new way of life. She even cautioned her that her selfish importunities could drive her son further away from her. Dan's mother did not try to contact her friend for a long period of time after this painful encounter. Fortunately, she began to realize how selfish her motives were, and gradually started to rise above her possessiveness and self-centeredness. Peace began to settle on both households.

Ever since he was a small youngster Ernie followed his father, John, as he went about the many chores on the family farm. When he became a teenager, he took pride in being able to perform some of these duties himself. Throughout the years, Ernie and his father developed a close relationship. It was by no means all work. Together they enjoyed fishing during the spring and summer, and hunting in the autumn season. Ernie also appreciated his parents' attendance at all the high school sporting events in which he took part.

A few months ago, Ernie left his home to begin his college education. His mother and father both experienced an emptiness in their life—something was missing in their household. For John the hours in the field became long and lonely. There was a tug in her heart as his mother set one less plate at the dinner table. John often said, "Just as the birds left their nest to fly south for the winter, so did Ernie, but thanks to Alexander Graham Bell we are able to visit with him over the phone."

PRACTICAL VACATIONS

Mark and Mary were grandparents whose nest was empty. Their fledglings had not only left home, but had flown to such distant cities as Dallas, Los Angeles, and San Francisco. Mark and Mary were resourceful grandparents and devised a plan to keep in touch with their sons and daughters and also to get to know their grandchildren as they were growing up. They decided to visit their children and grandchildren at different times of the year, especially if their visit could be helpful to the young parents. Their plan was a real boon. If the parents of their grandchildren wanted to get away for a vacation, or for some time alone, or even to make a business trip together, Mark and Mary would baby-sit for that period. Their plan was indeed a happy decision and welcomed by everyone concerned as it served several purposes at the same time. No empty-nest blues.

Grandparents must be careful to respect the discipline and house rules which the parents have set up. Their affection for their grandchildren may prompt them to relax the rules a bit or "spoil" them by granting them their every whim and wish. One young mother remarked that every time her parents visited them it took several weeks to "unspoil" her children again.

SPECIAL VISITS

Grandma T is the sole occupant in her otherwise empty nest, but she is by no means lonely. Her eight children are all married and nurturing families of their own. They left home some years ago. She says that her husband went off to heaven without taking her with him. There is a twinkle in her eye and a smile on her lips as she tells you about a daily visit with at least one of her own children, but especially with her grandchildren. It may not be a face-to-face visit, but it is a genuine visit nonetheless.

Grandma T takes some time each day to write a letter to a different son or daughter or grandchild. She admits that she enjoys writing to her grandchildren the most. She lets them know that she loves them very much and is very happy and proud to be their grandmother. Do they enjoy her letters? Indeed they do. In each letter she tells them about some capers which her children, their parents, did when they were growing up. She recalls the happy moments they enjoyed as a family and also some of the ups and downs that inevitably came their way. She goes back even further to share with them some of the "naughty" things she herself did as a child and teenager.

The grandchildren treasure her letters and are collecting them, assembling them into a diary. They may even become a family history. There is never a dull moment in Grandma T's life. Her empty nest gives her the time and space for her daily "visits."

NEW HORIZONS

In God's inscrutable plan, we are called to a personal ministry at various stages of our life. God invited us to a precise work which no one else could ever do in our place. Our motive in accepting the challenge will determine the level of fulfillment and satisfaction we will attain. If we recognize the invitation as God's will of preference for us, we will find great peace and contentment. On the other hand, if our motivation in reaching out to some person or worthy program is primarily self-satisfying, we will become a do-gooder without completely filling the void in our life. If we are motivated simply by selfishness, we will soon be disappointed and discouraged if we do not receive the recognition and thanks we expect.

Parents can prepare themselves for the time when their nest begins to empty out. This conditioning begins when they are blessed with their first child. Fathers and mothers should keep in mind that life is a gift from God and they are entrusted with a child to nurture and love this gift of God to them. In due time, they will be asked to give back to God his precious gifts by allowing their offspring to venture into the world to fulfill the missions to which God is calling them. During those wonderful years of loving, caring, providing for, and educating their children, parents do well to remind themselves that their children are only on loan to them for a short time. Enjoying their childhood and nurturing them into adulthood will bring much peace and satisfaction.

EVENING OF LIFE

There are endless possibilities available to combat an empty-nest syndrome. Parents give so much time and talent in raising their children without counting the cost. Love not only makes the burden bearable, but even a joy. The sacrifices parents make give them real satisfaction and feelings of accomplishment. When the nest becomes empty, they need to continue to give in order to find the same happiness and joy in giving themselves to others.

Hobbies are not only an enjoyable pastime, but can be beneficial in so many different ways. Parents often dream of having time to enjoy favorite hobbies, but rearing children leaves little opportunity. Hobbies can bring joy and satisfaction, and others too may profit from them.

I had the privilege of being associated with a priest who lost his eyesight at the age of fifty-nine and was not called to his heavenly home until he was eighty-seven. During those sightless years, he found a joyful spirit of accomplishment in taking up weaving as a hobby. His sisters would thread his looms while he worked out all kinds of devices to guide him in his weaving; a string of beads of different sizes, a series of little blocks guided him in every movement. He was able to weave a great variety of things such as tablecloths, handbags, place-mats, and priestly stoles. His hobby gave him no time to indulge in self-pity or boredom in his dark world.

Hobbies can be rewarding experiences for parents facing the empty-nest period in their lives, and can enable them to continue to give of themselves in many different ways. Many worthy causes are begging for volunteer help. Most parishes depend on a host of volunteers to build a dynamic Christian community, to help in the religious education program, and in other capacities. Countless other worthwhile programs depend on volunteer help without which they could not function. For the academically inclined, there are special college courses offered for senior citizens to further their education and their enjoyment of life.

Grandfather T.J. walks in the footsteps of St. Joseph by woodworking in his basement shop. He has been making little tables, doll beds, chests, and other furniture for his grandchildren. Many poor families have also benefited from his handiwork as he repairs or manufactures articles of furniture for them. Besides himself, many others have benefited from his hobby.

Barbara, a grandmother of young grandchildren, is an excellent seamstress. In past years her regular Christmas gift to the little ones was a pair of flannel pajamas which she sewed herself. More recently she has been helping her teenage grandchildren to sew and make some of their own clothing. She had to devise new patterns when she discovered the styles teenagers wear. She is looking forward to helping her granddaughters make their own wedding dresses.

Her hobby has also enriched other mothers who find a need to become more proficient in sewing for their young families. Barbara's only complaint is that her hands are not as nimble as they used to be.

Possibilities are endless for counteracting the empty-nest syndrome and bringing fulfillment and much joy into our lives.

PANACEA

Prayer is the most powerful antidote for relieving the symptoms of the empty-nest syndrome. It produces manifold fruits for both the immediate and extended family. Prayer is a great source of comfort to parents and a healing balm in moments of emptiness. A suggested procedure may be helpful in leading us into prayer.

Take time for a few moments each day to reflect on your life together as husband and wife down through the years. It was not accidental that you met, fell in love, and committed yourselves in marriage to each other, to God, and to your offspring. It was all in God's loving providence. Perhaps that is why we often say that some marriages are made in heaven.

A prayerful reflection will highlight the Lord's loving care and concern for you and your family. It will kindle deeper sentiments of gratitude and appreciation for the Lord's countless blessings. Faithfully spending time in prayerful reflection each day forms a habit of keeping you more deeply aware of the Lord's providential love hovering over your family for so many years. Repetition will aid you in forming such a habit. If you are ailing physically, normally one dose of medication will not cure the illness. It must be taken daily and consistently to bring relief or effect a cure. Likewise, praying daily will heal the emptiness in your heart.

Your prayer will include all the members of your family. Praying for each child and grandchild individually will help you recognize God's gifts in each one of them. Your prayer of petition for each one of them will mediate untold blessings for them. Implore the Lord daily to inspire and encourage, to guide and watch over them and, above all, to shower his love upon them. Lifting them up in prayer is one of the most precious gifts you can give your children and grandchildren.

Prayer has great bonding power. It will keep a family closely united in love, preparing them for difficulty or misunderstanding which may arise.

Prayer

Lord Jesus, you were the heart and soul of the Holy Family in Nazareth. By your presence in our family, fill us with your abundant love, forgiveness, and reconciliation. Strengthen us to face the challenges of each day. Grant us the grace to appreciate one another and to be eternally grateful to you. Amen

FOURTEEN

Divorce

Divorce ranks number one in most professional studies that rate the degree of personal anxiety and pain associated with a stressful life experience. It even ranks above the grief and emptiness of losing a loved one in death. The trauma of divorce is long-lived. Some divorcees carry pain to the grave. According to one study the severity of this painful stress diminishes somewhat for men in about two years, while women generally need about five years before the sharp edge of their stress wears off. The poet Milton speaks about the "wounds immedicable"—those that do not heal. Certainly the emotional suffering caused by divorce falls into this category.

When spouses face problems in their marriage and begin to feel that they are incompatible, they can easily be disillusioned by thinking that a divorce is the only solution to their difficulties. Little do they realize that a divorce will create a profusion of new and weightier problems, especially if there are children involved. Any person who has suffered through a divorce will quickly remind them that such a permanent separation will not usually restore the peace and tranquility expected and longed for.

Spouses, both during and after a divorce, experience painful emotional eruptions. If they are aware of the likelihood of these feelings arising within themselves, they will be better prepared to deal with them. The following are some of the stages they may pass through.

DISBELIEF

When a spouse threatens to get a divorce, or announces that he or she has filed for a divorce, often the other spouse cannot believe that such a tragedy could ever happen. They may consider it simply a threat so that the other party may win in a disagreement. After years of a rather stable marriage, they cannot possibly comprehend a valid reason for a divorce. They may regard it as some kind of bad dream or a horrible nightmare.

ANGER

When the legal apparatus is set into motion and the reality becomes more apparent, anger emerges. Anger is a reaction to anything threatening our personal security. Such a threat may come in the form of criticism, ridicule, rejection of our opinions, or questioning our intentions and motivation. How much more intense will be the anger when the marriage itself is threatened or terminated. When anger is aroused, we sometimes are unable to make prudent judgments. Anger can be so intense that it becomes irrational. Spouses who realize anger is a common emotion in a divorce proceeding will be less distraught at their own reaction and less fearful that they have lost their balance.

Added to her other vexing problems while going through her divorce, Sally was greatly disturbed by the anger that kept arising within her, causing her to explode for little or no rea-son. She shouted at her children and was sullen and discourte-ous with the people she met. She vented her anger toward her husband to anyone who would listen. In fact, she was mad at the whole world, as she put it, and even at God. She feared she was losing her emotional stability. When she learned that this was not an unexpected reaction under the circumstances, she was greatly relieved. Gradually, as the months passed, her dis-position changed and sunshine returned to her smile.

BLAME

When we are involved in a personal conflict, we are prone to point the finger of blame at someone else and to exonerate ourselves. To vindicate ourselves we are inclined to exaggerate the faults and shortcomings of the other person. Blaming the other person is a shield against an admission of our own culpa-bility. An honest appraisal of our own conduct and an admis-sion of our own faults would avoid many serious misunder-standings.

This is likewise the pattern in a marital crisis. Each spouse will usually try to place the burden of the blame on the partner for the breakup of their marriage. Each will blame the other for a lack of communication, cooperation, gratitude, and apprecia-tion, and a host of other faults which led to the fragmentation of the marriage. When anger blazes forth, a person may accuse his or her spouse, rightly or wrongly, of destructive behavior, anger, abuse, hatred, and even infidelity. Placing the full responsibility for the disruption in the marriage on the "of-fender" will help the accusing spouse justify seeking revenge in one form or another. The heartrending strain and disappoint-ment of going through a divorce process can warp a couple's judgment and render their thinking unreasonable.

REJECTION AND DEPRESSION

Persons going through a divorce often suffer deep depression. One of the contributing causes for this depression is the devastating feelings of rejection so common in divorce. The pain of rejection is most acute. Spouses who have placed all their trust and confidence in their partner and have shared their love totally without counting the cost, often discover that the feeling of rejection is their severest pain. When we love deeply, our vulnerability increases, making us susceptible to all the hurts and pains that divorce brings in its wake, especially the crushing feelings of rejection.

No one loved more intensely than did Jesus, thus making himself vulnerable. Centuries before he came into our world, the psalmist foretold the rejection that Jesus, the Messiah, would endure.

"If an enemy had reviled me,
    I could have borne it;
If he who hates me had vaunted against me,
    I might have hidden from him.
But you, my other self,
    My companion and my bosom friend!
You whose comradeship I enjoyed
    at whose side I walked."   Psalm 55:13-15

The painful rejection foretold by the psalmist became a reality with all its fierceness for Jesus in the Garden of Gethsemane when Judas handed him over to his enemies. How pathetic are the words of Jesus, "Judas, are you betraying the Son of Man with a kiss?" (Lk 22:48).

Having encountered rejection from so many quarters, Jesus understands the excruciating pangs a divorced person suffers. If we take our aching heart and rejected love to the Lord, we will find genuine comfort and consolation in his presence. He will fill our hearts with the warmth and sunshine of his boundless love to replace to overflowing the human love which we lost. His love will restore our dignity and self-image as we struggle to survive.

The pain of rejection and all the other anxieties will be mitigated as our thinking becomes more positive and we begin to rebuild our lives. A structure is built by placing one brick upon another. Likewise, restructuring our lives will also be a slow process, but each step brings us greater fulfillment and satisfaction.

ACCEPTANCE

Even though divorce brings untold heartache, the newly-divorced need to get on with their lives. We can begin with the realization that God loves us just as we are and that we are precious to him. He tells us that himself and we need to hear him say it to our heart (Is 43:4). We need to be consciously aware that "God is love" and has created us in his own image and likeness by sharing his loving nature with us. He has formed us with a desire to love and to be loved. When we know and experience that God loves us, we know that we are lovable and that gives us our real dignity as a person.

To assure us that he will never forget us, God tells us that he has written each of our names on the palm of his hand (Is 49:16). The Semitic understanding of this expression is a solemn confirmation that we will never be forgotten. How comforting is the Lord's promise that all is not lost, and that his loving providence remains forever with us! "For I know well the plans I have in mind for you, says the Lord, plans for your welfare, not for woe! Plans to give you a future full of hope" (Jer 29:11).

Jesus also reveals his love for us, "As the Father loves me, so I also love you" (Jn 15:9). We know that the Father loves Jesus with an infinite love and Jesus confirms the truth that he loves us with the same infinite love. Jesus also promised that he would never leave us, but would be with us at every moment of our life (Mt. 28:20). He abides with us always to soothe our heartaches, disappointments, our loneliness. He is with us to guide us, to enlighten us, and to help us in making decisions.

Pause many times throughout the day, especially when distressed, to visit briefly with the Lord who is present with us. We express our love for him by offering him the gift of ourselves which includes all that we have to endure throughout the day, not only the heartaches and concerns, but also the happy, peaceful moments. This is what Jesus meant when he said, "Remain in my love" (Jn 15:9). The awareness of the Lord's abiding presence with us always gives us great hope for the future. When we resolve to give him ourselves unstintingly by accepting his will for us, we will not only survive, but will be able to radiate the interior peace and joy he gives us to everyone around us, especially to the children whose hearts are heavy and who suffer such loss.

The following accounts may be a source of hope and encouragement to anyone on the road to survival. The people mentioned in these accounts move through several or all the reactions a person normally experiences when burdened with a grave loss. Different people will require shorter or longer periods of time to pass from one stage into another: from incredulity and disbelief into feelings of anger and frustration, then into a mood for bargaining and compromise, next into despondency and depression, and finally reaching the stage of resignation and acceptance.

SUE

Twelve years after suffering the trauma of going through a divorce, Sue wrote to a friend, recalling some of the pain and distress she suffered in the process. That pain lingers on for her even today. Although it was a crushing experience, Sue tells her friend how she was able to survive.

When Mike announced he was leaving me and my son, I was stunned. I just could not bring myself to believe the words I was hearing. It hit me so hard that within six weeks I lost twenty pounds; food made me ill. I kept searching through the years of marriage asking myself what I had done wrong. What should I have done and neglected to do?

I pleaded with Mike to stay and not break up our marriage and family life. I told him I would do whatever he wanted. He assured me that I had done nothing wrong and that I should not blame myself for what he was about to do. Then I became very angry. I was angry at myself for my futile begging. I was angry with Mike for thinking only of himself and not of his wife and our eight-year-old son who idolized his father. Yes, I was angry even at God and questioning his love and care for us.

After some time the picture became clear to me. I was merely a stepping stone in Mike's life. He said that when we were married, he was a "T-shirt and blue jeans" country kid. He was honest in saying that he married me as an opportunity to better his social and economic status. After these twelve years of marriage he found another woman who could help him even more. She could help him financially and also introduce him to some elite people. With that in mind, he left my son and me and immediately began divorce proceedings.

My life was a frazzle. The pain of rejection was excruciating. I thought my heart would break. It hurt to think that he used me only as a stepping stone. Once when I tried to persuade him, he replied, "Life is unfair so I have to take advantage of opportunities when they present themselves, no matter who gets hurt." The thought of being rejected almost crushed me. My resentment and bitterness knew no bounds. When all this was happening, I did not think I could go on.

Unwittingly, my son came to my rescue. When I saw how

much he was hurting and missing his daddy, I realized that I was focusing too much on myself. With the hurt he was experiencing, I understood that I must be his port in the storm. I had to put my life back together for his sake.

In striving to recover from this devastating experience, I found my real anchor was the Lord. As I tried to reach above the concern I had for myself, the thought occurred to me that the Lord loves me, and would never reject me. Knowing that his love is secure helped me to raise myself up by my bootstraps. As I was praying one day, I reflected on the truth that no one loved more than the Lord himself, thus making himself very vulnerable. The utter rejection Jesus suffered was far greater than mine could ever be. He was well aware of my suffering. I also recalled that he promised he would be with us always and that he would never leave us orphans. I started to go to Mass every day when possible. Many times I could not hear the prayers at Mass as my sobs and tears flowed copiously. One day our good pastor read the Gospel at Mass in which Jesus invites us to come to him when we are burdened and we will find rest for our souls (Mt 11:28). That is exactly what I needed to hear to encourage me to start rebuilding my life.

Throughout all my struggles, my family and friends have been loyal and supportive. They walked all the way with me as I travelled through the desert of loneliness, frustration and pain. After twelve years the hurt is still there, but is gradually diminishing. I am also finding more comfort and consolation and I am more at peace.

Sue is finding peace of mind and heart since she is striving to forgive and forget. She is thinking more positively as she rebuilds her life. Her favorite prayer, which she has prayed thousands of times, is, "Lord, heal me and help me forgive."

Unlike Sue, Lisa, age thirty-one, has found it impossible to forgive her mother. She has not spoken to her mother for many years, and has never forgiven her mother for divorcing her father so that she could pursue her own career. Lisa was thirteen at the time and has since lived with her father. Until Lisa tries to forgive, she will never be a genuinely happy person at peace with herself and with others.

GEORGE AND MARTHA

I knew George and Martha for many years. To all external appearances, they seemed to be happily married, even though the usual little disagreements crept up from time to time. They seemed to resolve their differences in stride. I was shocked recently when I learned that Martha was suing for a divorce. I was even more distressed when I was informed of the reasons she alleged for getting a divorce. She said that after thirty years of marriage and caring for the family she wanted a new lease and outlook on life. This was promised to her by her employer who was in the process of divorcing his own wife. He assured Martha that he could fulfill her desire for a new life if she would marry him. George unsuccessfully tried to reason with his wife of thirty years, assuring her that all her needs could be satisfied if she would share her wants and desires with him and their adult children.

When George and I conversed about his plight, he said that his worst anguish and deepest hurt was in being rejected and losing the best friend and companion he had ever known. He could not comprehend how she was willing to give up her family for a divorced man. He was grieved over the betrayal of the marital trust and confidence which was the cornerstone of their marriage. George was also hurt by his wife's disloyalty and the patterns of deceit which were beginning to come to light.

George was saddened as their children were becoming more and more alienated from their mother. They were deeply wounded for they had loved their mother over the years and could not understand what was happening to her now that she was deserting them. They were becoming more supportive of their father, but he would not permit them to criticize their mother nor make any derogatory remarks about her. He kept reminding his adult children to continue to love her and to pray fervently for her.

Years later, guilt seems to weigh heavily on Martha's conscience. She comes to visit George regularly, and calls the children weekly, even though two of them live in distant cities. Her married daughter has asked her mother not to call anymore, since her calls always have the same purpose: attempting to justify her decision in getting a divorce and assuring her children how very happy she is in her new home.

George has taken several steps in trying to adjust to a lonely way of life. He sold their large home filled with so many happy memories, and moved into a much smaller home. He confessed that it is very hard to come home to an empty house. George firmly believes that God can bring some good out of this crisis.

George is a college professor and has taken on more classes and speaking engagements to keep his mind occupied, in spite of the unhappy reality of spending the rest of his life alone. He is also working on a manuscript for a book he has dreamed about for many years; his evenings are often spent in studying and writing. Even though he enjoys academic work and derives a great amount of satisfaction from it, he admits that the hurt, the disappointment, and the feelings of rejection accompany him every day.

George says that he has become a more prayerful person and, as he prays for his wife, tears well up and flow freely. His final comment was, "Others have made it alone, and with the good Lord's help, I will keep trudging on along."

CHILDREN AND DIVORCE

We are becoming more aware and concerned about the devastating effects divorce has on all the members of a family, especially on emotionally vulnerable children. When parents are divorced, children are the innocent victims. Parents are often too preoccupied with their own personal fear, pain, rejection and anger with each other to be fully aware of the turmoil and suffering their children are enduring. Parents may not be able to comfort and reassure their children or help them adjust more easily to the new family structure.

There is never a "good age" at which children can experience a divorce of their parents without being deeply and emotionally affected. Younger children often feel at fault, while older children usually take sides with one parent or the other.

SECURITY

Younger children suffer a loss of their security. The greatest security they can have is to know that their mother and father love each other and that they also love them and want them close. Divorce means that some of this love no longer protects them adequately. Younger children react in various ways. Their pain is reflected in lack of interest in school, in angry outbursts, in recurring moodiness, and other unhealthy behavior patterns.

GUILT

Younger children may be plagued with a sense of guilt, that somehow they were the cause of the unrest in the home and the reason their father or mother left. They express these feelings in different ways. An eight-year-old boy asked his mother, "Did Daddy go away because I was naughty and did not do what he told me?" Before his mother could respond, he blurted out, "If you put me in an orphanage, will Daddy come back?" Parents can alleviate some of their children's guilt feelings by reassuring them that life will go on in spite of major changes at home. Parents can comfort them and explain that they will always love them as their special children. Children want to know they are loved. They are delighted to learn that Jesus loves them and they are very precious to him. What reassurance parents can give them by telling them how Jesus asked little children to come to him that he might embrace and bless them (Mk 10:13-16)! In a convincing way, they can reassure the children that they are not responsible for the marriage breakup.

EMBARRASSMENT

Children of divorce are easily embarrassed when playmates and school chums chat about life at home with their mothers and fathers. They are ashamed to admit that their mom or dad does not live at home anymore. These children need to know there are other homes besides theirs with only one parent.

A popular sixth-grade teacher resigned his position at the peak of his professional career, much to the disappointment of the administration, the staff and parents of the children. He confided that twenty-six of his twenty-seven pupils came from single-parent homes. He could not endure the heartache when children would cling to him, no doubt seeing a father image in him. In many urban schools, over half of the students come from single-parent homes. Fortunately, counseling programs and workshops are being set up for both children and parents, helping them to cope with the emotional pain and distress resulting from divorce.

LONELINESS

Young children of divorced parents feel greatly deprived when they see the presence and interaction of other parents with their children, compared to their own sad conditions. Big Brothers and Big Sisters organizations generously try to fill some of this loneliness and deprivation with the programs they plan for these needy children. Their efforts are needed and commendable, but they cannot fully make up for the emptiness in the hearts of their charges.

VISITATION

Visiting with the absent parent, usually the father, can be a two-way street. It can either foster real bonding, or it can compound problems and cause the children more distress. It can be an occasion for an absent parent to manifest his care and concern for the children, assuring them of his personal love by showing interest in their schooling and encouraging them to work at their education. An absent father can be a great support by encouraging the children to follow their mother's instructions and be helpful at home. He can tell his children how proud he is of them when they are good and do what their mother asks of them. Such visits can be very fruitful. Visits with an absent parent can bring much good, reminding the children that both parents love them.

On the other hand, visiting with the parent not living at home can be a bad experience for children, especially if asked about their other parent's activities: *Is he going out with anyone? Is she good to you? Are your meals well prepared? Does he get angry often? What does she say about me?* Such interrogation is severely damaging to their young minds.

Visiting with the father can take on a holiday atmosphere which can be equally harmful. He may try to buy his children's affection and loyalty by granting them all their childish wishes. Showering them with gifts and gadgets that the custodial parent (usually the mother) cannot responsibly afford, can undermine the other parent's authority. Extravagant spending manifests the absent parent's insecurity and guilt feelings about the divorce. It also leaves the children disgruntled about going back home to the routine, work and challenges of living more realistically with the custodial parent.

When the mother has custody of the children, she has to discipline them from time to time, but may not be able to give them the things they want, as the father tries to do. The children can be further confused and the mother's problems are intensified. Even when husband and wife attempt to continue a friendly relationship, it can be a way of denying the conflict that caused the separation. Children cannot understand why their parents are not living together to re-establish a happy home. Indeed, young children become the innocent victims of a broken home, deprived of the peace and security they need and deserve.

OLDER CHILDREN

Older children, even those no longer living at home, suffer intensely when their parents are divorced. The disappointment and stress may not be as detrimental as it is for younger children, but it is very painful nonetheless.

When divorce occurs, older sons and daughters are often angry, especially at the one they think is more responsible for the breakup. If a third party is involved, their anger is even greater. They are angry with themselves, feeling guilty for the things they have done in years past which might have contributed to their parents' decision.

Older sons and daughters usually ponder what they can and should do about the situation. Reason with their parents? Their parents disagreed frequently and violently in these last few years, making threats to one another, but the sons and daughters regarded them only as idle threats to achieve their own will in a disagreement.

These siblings become depressed in the face of their parents' divorce, frustrated and helpless in this crisis, and embarrassed among their peers. How will they continue contact with either or both of their parents, even though their respect for them is challenged? Young adults find it difficult to remain impartial, especially when both parents are vying for their love and loyalty. This inner struggle is born of appreciation for all their parents have done for them.

Older children are more apt to take sides, realizing who took the initiative and who is more responsible for the divorce. The spouse who experiences the most guilt will often strive to keep the affection and loyalty of the children. Whether the attempt is obvious or more subtle, children are usually aware of such tactics, alienating them more from one or both parents.

BOOMERANG

The divorced person often experiences a sense of guilt and failure. Trying to prove that his or her action was good for all concerned may create considerable friction and tension, even in events which should be times of joy and celebration. The following is an actual account of how far-reaching such attempts can be.

Joe and Nancy were planning their wedding and were looking forward to a happy and joyous celebration. Nancy's parents were divorced and both were remarried. Nancy's mother insisted on taking care of the design and printing of the wedding invitations. She used this occasion as an opportunity to prove to her friends and acquaintances that her divorce and remarriage was a wise decision for both herself and her ex-husband. The announcement was designed something like this:

"Mr. and Mrs. Smith (Nancy's mother and stepfather)
and
"Mr. and Mrs. Jones (Nancy's father and stepmother)
request the honor of your presence...."

The parents of the groom were not even mentioned. The

excuse offered by Nancy's mother was that the announcement would be too crowded. Needless to say, it caused Joe and Nancy great pain and frustration. Joe's parents were naturally surprised and shocked. Fortunately they are good Christians and concealed their disappointment by making light of the situation in order not to cast a shadow on this happy occasion.

This is just one of the many tensions and embarrassments which can result from a divorce. Had the bride's mother not been feeling pangs of guilt and failure, this probably would not have happened. This determined action on the part of Nancy's mother boomeranged and further alienated Nancy from her mother. On the other hand, it increased Nancy's admiration for her new in-laws and their gracious understanding and kindness to her.

LOOKING BEYOND THE LOSS

Parents will often vie for the loyalty of their grown children by trying to justify their divorce. This creates great difficulty for their young adult children. There is a very fine line between condemning and condoning. It is hard for them not to show any partiality, even though their hearts are inclined to reach out to one or the other parent. As time moves on, the children may experience some relief as the frustration and disappointment seem to diminish.

Pauline explained her survival technique in these words, "In the first place, I will not permit either my mother or father to speak to me about my other parent. When the thought of my parents abandoning each other in divorce bothers me, I offer a little prayer for them asking God to bless them and grant them peace of mind and heart. I also ask the Lord's forgiveness if any of my actions or attitudes in the past have been in any way responsible for the failure of my parents' marriage. I thank him for all my parents have done for me all through the years. Their breakup made me realize the importance of communication and a willingness to listen in solving problems in and out of marriage."

GRANDPARENTS

Reverberations of a broken marriage expand in ever-widening circles beyond the immediate family. Grandparents are deeply disappointed and unhappy when the marriage of a son or daughter ends in divorce. They are naturally concerned for and anxious about the future of the divorced couple and even more concerned about their grandchildren and worried about the damage that they will endure.

Grandparents, too, can be plagued with a sense of guilt, wondering if they neglected to prepare their son or daughter sufficiently for the ups and downs of marriage. During the stormy years they tried not to interfere in their conflict. Now they are wondering if they did the right thing. With their years of experience they might have prevented a total disruption.

Grandparents can still play an important role. They can affirm their grandchildren by showing an interest in all they do, by assuring them that they are loved and lovable, and encouraging them to look forward and prepare for the great future which awaits them. Grandfathers can project a masculine model for the children, especially to the boys by taking an active interest in their games and activities. Grandmothers can support and implement the mothers' care and concern for their children. Together they can give grandchildren a sense of security and importance. Such prudent concern will also help alleviate the grandparents' worry and anxiety and bring them much relief.

Prayer

Father, we place in your loving care all the hurt children of divorced couples. Heal their heartaches, keep them close to you, never let them stray from you as they journey through life. Amen

FIFTEEN

Death and Dying

As I was being seated at a luncheon meeting, at which I was to speak to a woman's organization, I overheard a person saying to her friends sitting at table with her: "Today we are not going to mention anything about serious illness of any kind, much less anything about death." For some people the fear of death has been an obsession; they may talk relentlessly of their aches and pains. For others it is almost paralyzing fear, to be forgotten at all costs. We often speak about death in euphemisms such as passing, being laid to rest, departing life, or entering life. Some concern about death is conducive to help us live a Christian way of life. It is only natural to be concerned about the unknown aspects of death such as its finality, no turning back, no second chance. Publishers have capitalized on our insatiable curiosity about life hereafter and have flooded our newsstands and book racks with apocalyptic literature that arouses our curiosity, but sheds no further light on this great unknown.

Jesus speaks about his own death as his glorification. He taught us to consider death as a doorway leading into our own glorification. Jesus did not give us a detailed description of life hereafter, but he did teach us how to live to attain the eternal life awaiting us.

COPING WITH THE DEATH OF A LOVED ONE

When the Lord calls someone near and dear to us to his or her eternal reward, we naturally experience a period of mourning. Tears may flow freely, sorrow fills our heart, grief grips our soul. In our distress we experience an emptiness, a loneliness, a sadness. These feelings are natural human reactions as we go through a period of mourning. During such a painful time, we need to remember that no suffering is in vain for the Lord knows every ache of our heart. The Jews used a quaint expression to remind themselves that God knew their weeping and would requite it for he carefully collected all their tears in a bottle. "My tears are stored in your flask; are they not recorded in your book?" (Ps 56:9).

It is gratifying to see a survivor often visiting the grave of a loved one to renew his or her affection, to commune in spirit, to offer a prayer for eternal peace. It is a custom that narrows the gap of loneliness and softens the pain.

When a loved one dies, various reactions may occur within us and in the lives of those around us. Observing other people's reactions will help us understand our own feelings.

Incredulity. Our first reaction may be disbelief. We cannot immediately comprehend it when those who are dear to us leave us forever. For some time after their death, we may still be expecting to find them in their accustomed place.

Ned loved his elderly mother and called her every day and visited her often, even though she was in good health and able to live alone. One morning at work, he received a call informing him that his mother had died in her sleep. Ned was well aware that his mother had seen many summers, but he could not comprehend her not being there when he called or visited.

The suddenness of her death shocked him. For months afterwards, he would pick up the phone to call her and then realize she was no longer there. Ned was passing through the stage of disbelief.

Joe and Mary were stunned when the sheriff brought them the shocking news that their son was killed in a one-car traffic accident. They could not believe that this was true—there must be a mistake. He had just left them a short time before to return to his college dorm. They could not comprehend that such a tragedy happened. They were incredulous.

Anger. As we strive to comprehend the reality of the death of a loved one, we normally experience feelings of anger arising within us. We are prone to become angry when events go contrary to our will, or when someone disagrees with us. Any threat to our security, our way of thinking, or our complacency will often elicit an angry response in us. Anger drains our energy, warps our thinking, and obscures our vision. When death robs us of a loved one, feelings of anger may be enkindled within us. They may even be directed at God. We begin to doubt his loving concern for us. It may cause our faith to waver as it robs us of the peace we once experienced.

Our next reaction may be feelings of distress and disappointment that we have dared to permit ourselves to become angry at God. Acknowledging our anger is the first step toward overcoming this undesirable reaction within us. In due time, we can be certain that our anger will wane.

Depression. Some good people anguish so deeply over the loss of someone dear to them that they become clinically depressed. This type of depression is a crippling malady robbing us of our ability to function normally. It causes us to isolate ourselves from family and friends, to lose interest in living—it deprives us of genuine peace and joy. A person suffering from depression is helpless and needs understanding love, support, and wholesome counseling.

After her husband left her, Pearl made a serious effort to be a good parent and keep her household intact despite the heavy burden she was carrying. A devastating blow sent her into depression when her only son with diagnosed with leukemia. When her son died some time later, Pearl's depression worsened. She managed to hold on to her job, thanks to an understanding employer, but nothing else in life interested her. She seemed to be in a daze at times. The wise counseling of her pastor eventually started her on the road to recovery.

Bargaining. In a longer or shorter period of time, anger and depression will eventually begin to wane, especially as we realize that our loved one is enjoying the unimaginable peace and happiness of heaven. As the pain of loss is mitigated, we are inclined to strike some sort of bargain with the Lord. We tell the Lord that we will try to accept the loss of the person we love, if God will grant us a certain request.

When cancer claimed the life of his dear wife, Theresa, Paul became frustrated and angry at God for taking her away from him and their three young children who needed a mother. *Why? Why? Why?*, he muttered endlessly. He was upset with himself because he did not want to experience these disturbing feelings toward God.

As time passed, Paul moved away from his angry stage into a bargaining with God. He begged God to give him the grace, strength, and wisdom to know how to care for his family. With God's help, he promised to keep the family together and to bring the children up as good Christians. After several years, Paul stated that God was keeping his end of the bargain and he was doing his best to keep his commitment.

After fifty years of the couple's happily married life, God called Angie's husband to his eternal reward. The separation and adjustment was most difficult for her. She was always a happy, cheerful person and did not want her attitude to change, burdened as she was with grief. She told the Lord that she would do her best to accept her loss, provided the Lord did not allow her to become an unhappy, miserable woman. She also asked the Lord to fill her loneliness and emptiness with a deeper sense of his personal presence with her. Angie successfully reached her bargaining stage.

Acceptance. Reaching a plateau of acceptance is the fifth and last stage in our struggle with the loss of a loved one in death. The process cannot be hurried; it takes time; in some cases considerable time, even years. Acceptance of God's will does not imply that times of pain, sorrow, and loneliness will not recur, but it does enable us, regardless of the heartache, to say yes to the Lord.

Cancer claimed the life of Louis, the twenty-two-year-old son of John and Lena. It was a stunning blow to both of his parents, especially since he had just reached the prime of his life. Lena was deeply grieved; over and over she relived the endless hours spent at his bedside during his dreadful illness. During the months that followed, she experienced all the stages of grief, until she finally was able to accept God's will. After she was able to let go, she began to experience some peace and consolation.

Each year the anniversary of Louis' death is a painful, tear-filled time for both parents. They wonder if they have really acquiesced to God's will, since such painful memories continue to plague them. Lena says she is not certain she has accepted God's plan in taking Louis, since now and then doubts arise in her heart. When rebellion stirs within her, she goes in spirit to stand with Mary under the cross of Jesus on Calvary. There she finds comfort and peace. In no way do these returning feelings mean she is resisting the Lord's will. We need to remember that feelings do not invalidate our will.

Jesus always shows us the way. In the Garden of Gethsemane he cringed at the prospect of the cruel suffering which lay ahead, but the resolve of his will prompted him to say, "Father, not my will but yours be done" (Lk 22:42). Jesus was consistent in his obedience to the Father (2 Cor 1:19).

Mary's model. It is possible that no pain was more severe and no acceptance was given more completely than in Mary's oblation as she stood by the cross of Jesus on that first Good Friday. Excruciating as was her suffering, her heart was in tune with the Father's will. This is evident from her standing quietly on Calvary's hill. She did not swoon in grief, nor did she cry out at the injustice of the sentence, nor did she threaten the executioners. Mary's "standing" manifests her total acquiescence to God's will. She is rightly called the Mother of Sorrows, but she is also the Mother of Consolation for each of us.

My two mothers. God called my mother to her heavenly home when I was twelve years old, the second oldest of six children. The baby of our family was only six months at the time. Even at this early age, I experienced the pangs of emptiness, loneliness, and growing feelings of anger against God. I missed my mother awakening us in the morning, advising us what to wear for school that day. I felt sad when I arrived home with no fragrance of newly baked bread permeating the kitchen and no welcoming arms of my mother. My father did a masterful job of keeping our family together, striving to be both mother and father to us. I experienced another severe pain when I caught my father crying—especially when one of us said something about Mother.

As the weeks went by I grew more angry at God, at life, at the doctor who let my mother die. I had no interest in school, nor did I care to play with my friends. One day when I screamed my hatred of everything, my father advised me to go to my room and pray for Mother. As I threw myself on the bed, suddenly the words of my mother came back to me. From her hospital bed on the day she died she said to me, "I am not going back home with you, but don't worry, for now you will have two mothers in heaven! When you run into difficulty or need to make a decision, talk it over first with your two mothers and we will be there to help you." This is the first time her words came back to me since she died. As I explained my feelings to both my mothers (my own mother and our Mother Mary), I became more peaceful and my anger seemed to wane. Many times through the next years, I recalled my mother's advice and things seemed to go more smoothly.

Some years later, I was summoned home from college because of the severity of my father's illness brought on by cancer. All the old feelings of anger, disappointment, and loneliness were aroused once again within me. I just could not understand why God was devastating our family, especially as we had grown very close to each other since my mother's death. In my self-pity, the void and emptiness of life kept me very depressed. Once again, my mother's dying words came back to me. I had not gone to Mary, the Mother of Jesus, and my own dear mother, to ask their help in this latest crisis, but only focused on myself. Once again, as I prayed to both of them to help me, I was able to find peace and joy. Now when I think of my parents, I thank God for them and rejoice with the peace and happiness they are enjoying together with the Lord and his Mother.

To this day I still call upon both of my mothers when a little crisis comes up or when I am faced with a big decision.

REFLECTING ON OUR OWN DEATH

Most of us are reluctant to think about our own death and even less anxious for the time of death to arrive in the near future. We are constantly striving to prolong life and delay the time of death as long as possible. Like a tiny tot we choose a shiny dime rather than a $100 bill. Our whole life from birth onward is a struggle to ward off death. We fear death for various reasons: we are loathe to leave our loved ones who depend on us; we fear the unknown; we dread the sufferings which often precede death. We seldom reflect on the eternal bliss the Lord wishes to give us.

A minister once asked all those in the congregation who

wanted to go to heaven to stand. As expected the whole congregation rose to their feet. Next he asked all those who
wanted to go to hell to remain standing and the rest to sit. One
man alone remained standing. Somewhat surprised, the minister asked, "Do you really want to go to hell?" "No," the man
replied, "but I did not want to see you standing all alone."

Everyone I know wants to go to heaven, but I do not know
anyone who relishes dying as the means of going there. Nor
does the average person want to leave this world just yet. We
have a fear of suffering and dying because we cannot comprehend even slightly the eternal joy and happiness awaiting us.
Nor do we recall that death is only a doorway through which
we pass in order to be united with our Father in perfect love
and peace.

Uncertain about getting into heaven. Do you worry that
you will not accomplish all the good in life that you would like
to have done? Are you troubled when you reflect on all the
opportunities you had to do some good, but you let them pass
by without doing anything? Are you upset because you did not
do anything very important in this world? Do you regard other
people as better and holier than you and therefore deserving a
heavenly reward while your efforts accomplished so little?

These tormenting thoughts creep into our minds because we
are influenced by the society in which we live. In our consumer-
oriented society, a person is judged not by who he is as a person, but rather by what he has accomplished. Mistakenly, we
think that God judges us in the same way—by what we have
accomplished and not by who we are. We have fashioned God
as a divine bookkeeper.

Scripture eradicates this false notion of earning our eternal
salvation. St. Paul tells us that we cannot merit our eternal
reward, but that it is a gift from God. We must be open and
cooperative in preparing ourselves to receive that divine gift.
He is very emphatic when he says, "By grace you have been
saved through faith, and this is not from you; it is the gift of

God, it is not from works" (Eph 2:8f). Reflecting on this sublime truth turns our anxieties into a spirit of gratitude and
praise for God's merciful love.

Faith eradicates fear. It is only natural for us to harbor some
fear of the great unknown beyond the door of death. Even
though we have many reassurances from the Lord, our trust
level cannot eliminate all anxieties. Jesus tells us not to let our
hearts be troubled, but to have faith in him, for he is going to
prepare a place for us. How comforting are his words, "I will
come back again and take you to myself, so that where I am
you also may be" (Jn 14:3ff).

On another occasion Jesus tells us the reason for his coming
into the world, "I came that they might have life and have it
more abundantly" (Jn 10:10). If we still have some lingering
doubts about our salvation, the divine promise of Jesus should
wipe them out. "I will not reject anyone who comes to me.... I
shall raise him on the last day" (Jn 6:37ff).

Our faith and trust level will be greatly increased when
Scripture assures us, "For God so loved the world that he gave
his only Son, so that everyone who believes in him might not
perish but might have eternal life" (Jn 3:16). These words reit-
erate what Jesus has already told us. They leave no room for
fear because perfect love casts out all fear.

Our heavenly Mother is vitally concerned about our eternal
happiness, since she does not want a single soul, redeemed by
her Son, to be lost. To assure us of her maternal, loving concern, God has permitted her to appear many times to guide us
on our earthly pilgrimage and keep our path directed heavenward. With faith and confidence we pray constantly, "Pray for
us sinners now and at the hour of our death."

By his own example, Jesus clarified the purpose and the need
for our dying. He took on our human nature by becoming
man, assuming a body like ours, so that he could take us down
to death with him to redeem us and give us the potential to
receive his divine life. He rose from the dead to share his risen,

exalted life with us to the extent that we are capable of receiving it. St. Paul emphasized this truth when he explains that our baptism is a dying and rising with Christ so that "we, too, may live in the newness of life" (Rom 6:3ff). At the moment of our death when we will no longer be inhibited by our human body, we will be gifted with the Lord's divine life and love in all its fullness.

A brighter view of death. The dying and rising of Jesus, in order to redeem us, opens up a whole new understanding of death. At one time we thought of death as a violent wrenching of the soul from the body to take its flight alone to the judgment seat of God. This understanding of death naturally filled us with a great fear of dying.

There is a more comfortable and consoling way to envision death. At the time of our baptism the Lord took up his dwelling within us. St. Paul's question is a reminder to us: "Do you not know that you are the temple of God, and that the spirit of God dwells in you?" (1 Cor 3:16). Jesus promised that he would always be with us and within us and never leave us (Jn 14:17).

The Lord loves us with an infinite, unconditional love. Genuine love is mutual; it wants to share life and love with the beloved. In redeeming us, Jesus enabled us to share in his divine love, but only in a limited degree, since our spirit is encumbered by our human body. At the time of death, we leave our human body so that our spirit might be more fully united with the Lord in bonds of a more perfect love and life. Nor is death a lonely experience. Jesus promised to remain with us always, and that does not exclude the moment of death. We can be certain that he is accompanying us as we cross the chasm into eternity.

The resurrection was one of the themes about which St. Paul preached so often and so eloquently. He tells us that which is corruptible must clothe itself with incorruptibility and likewise that which is mortal must clothe itself with immortality. When this happens through the transforming power of God, then Paul bids us rejoice for "then the word that is written shall come about:

Death is swallowed up in victory.
Where, O death, is your victory?
Where, O death, is your sting?"   **1 Corinthians 15:54f**

Prayer for a Happy Death

Father, you made us in your own image and your Son accepted death for our salvation. Help us to keep watch in prayer at all times. May we be free from sin when we leave this world and rejoice in peace with you forever. We ask this through our Lord Jesus Christ, your Son, who lives and reigns with you and the Holy Spirit, one God, forever and ever. Amen

SIXTEEN

I Will Give You Rest

Earl had lived a happy, fulfilled life. The years had flown so quickly that he now found himself a senior citizen. All through the years, Earl had tried to live a good Christian life, dealing honestly with others, helping whenever and wherever he was needed. Yet Earl was deeply troubled and worried about one aspect of his past life:

> Every time I think about my past life, I get worried and discouraged when I recall some of the things I have done. Even though I tried to do what I thought was right, I failed the Lord more times than I can count. Far too often I went off on a tangent away from the straight and narrow path I was supposed to follow as a Christian. I sinned many times and there were some real whoppers, too. When I think back, I wonder if God really did forgive me. I wonder if I was sorry enough to have them forgiven? Will God hold them against me on Judgment Day? How can I know for sure that my sins are forgiven?

REVIEWING OUR OWN LIFE

Can we identify with Earl? Do similar memories, doubts, and fears plague us from time to time? My response to Earl was a brief reassurance that he belonged to the same human race in which we all claim membership, with all our errant escapades, all our broken resolves, all our repeated falls in spite of our best intentions.

Many of us have probably experienced the same concern and anxiety about our own sinfulness in the past. Why should these bygone escapades plague us in later years? For one reason, as we add a few years to our life span, our thoughts naturally turn more frequently to the past. We relive many of our experiences of years ago.

EVIL ONE AT WORK

The devil is well aware of our tendency to recall our past life so marred with some regrets. This is his trump card and a powerful tool in trying to lead us into the temptation to become discouraged and even to despair. The devil realizes that if we get discouraged, we will give up and no longer try to live a life close to the Lord.

When we reflect on the years gone by, the evil one would remind us that we are not so good and that we are living a life of hypocrisy. He taunts us about our sinful falls. He enkindles doubts, fears, and anxieties within us, knowing that if he can get us discouraged we will give up.

OUR REACTION

How should we react to these wiles of the evil one? In the first place, we must simply order him out of our thoughts and feelings. The devil does not mind if we curse him, since our deprecations will take our thoughts away from the Lord, but he does not want to be laughed at. Laughing at his futile efforts to get us discouraged will be a big step toward healing.

Next we turn to the Lord and praise and thank him for his infinite mercy, compassion, and enduring willingness to forgive us regardless of who we are or what we have done. Our loving Father wants to forgive us more than we could want to be forgiven. How is that possible? His love is infinite and given freely to anyone in need of it.

JESUS FORGIVES

We find great comfort and reassurance in recalling the loving mercy and forgiveness of Jesus to all the sinners who came to him during his earthly sojourn. The woman taken in adultery immediately comes to mind—she experienced the forgiveness of Jesus (Jn 8:1-11). The sinful woman in the Pharisee's house experienced the peace and pardon which Jesus so eagerly granted her (Lk 7:36-50). How willing Jesus was to heal the leper who sought his mercy (Lk 5:12-15)! In none of these cases did Jesus ask for any lengthy acknowledgment of their wrongdoing. He recognized the dispositions of their hearts filled with sincere, humble sorrow for their misdeeds and immediately pardoned them.

Who cannot be deeply moved by the tender mercy of Jesus extended to the criminal being crucified with him? The criminal asked only to be remembered when Jesus came into his kingdom. He not only received an assurance of a remembrance, but a divine promise that he would be with Jesus in paradise that very day (Lk 23:39-43). How comforting is the prayer of Jesus from his deathbed on the cross, "Father, forgive them; they know not what they do" (Lk 23:34). We are also included in that prayer of Jesus for he came to save every person. Furthermore, Scripture assures us that Jesus who is the same yesterday, today, and forever is always willing to forgive (Heb 13:8).

Our fears and doubts about the Lord's forgiveness of our past sins arise from our weak faith and a lack of confidence and trust in our gracious God. We may firmly believe that he will forgive everyone else except ourselves. How convincing are the words of Jesus, "Amen, I say to you, all sins and all blasphemies that people utter will be forgiven them" (Mk 3:28). Any time Jesus found faith he healed and forgave all sins. These episodes from the Gospel are only a few of the many times Jesus reached out with his forgiving love. These few should convince us that if we are sorry, he will forgive and has forgiven our sinfulness. To increase our faith and trust in the Lord's forgiveness, we ought to pray the same words uttered by the father of the demon-possessed boy, "I do believe, help my unbelief" (Mk 9:24).

CHANNELS OF PEACE AND PARDON

Jesus knew how much we would agonize over our past sins because of our lack of faith in him. He understood the unfounded tendency of our human nature to doubt his mercy and forgiveness. To allay these anxieties that rob us of the peace and joy Jesus came to bring us, he instituted two powerful channels to convey his redemptive love to each one of us personally and individually. The first of these unique channels is the Sacrament of Reconciliation and the second is the Sacrifice of the Mass.

In the Sacrament of Reconciliation, as well as in all other sacraments, we encounter the Person of Jesus. He awaits our coming in the sacrament to acknowledge honestly and humbly our sinfulness, to be receptive to his boundless forgiving love and to be resolved to avoid sin to the best of our ability in the future.

A brief reflection of the role that Jesus continues to fulfill in our lives will bring us to a deeper appreciation of his forgiving love. It will also strengthen our faith and build up our trust and confidence in him. Jesus came into the world to be our Savior and Redeemer. Now he is in his glory, but what is his glory? His glory is simply continuing his redemptive work among us by forgiving and healing all who meet him in the Sacrament of Reconciliation. When we encounter Jesus in this sacrament, he is greatly pleased, since by our actions and attitude we acknowledge our need for him as Savior and Redeemer. Our faith assures us that the Lord is abiding with us and within us. His presence is not a static presence, but a dynamic, operative presence cleansing us and picking us up every time we fall.

Jesus is also our healer. We need a healing along with forgiveness. By way of an example, if we are critical and judgmental, or find it difficult to forgive another person, or harbor a resentment toward someone, we need the Lord's healing from the pride or insecurity which is responsible for our critical attitude. His divine, healing power will transform our feelings and attitudes if we cooperate with his healing presence.

Bill had just enjoyed a good spaghetti dinner and decided to pay a visit to his pastor to seek some advice about his anxiety over past sins. He asked, "How can I be sure that God has forgiven me my sinfulness?" His good pastor saw the spaghetti stain on his clean shirt and asked Bill, "Since you stained your shirt are you going to throw it away?" Bill was quick to reply that a good washing would make it like new again. His pastor capitalized on his response. "Neither does God throw us away when we stain our soul."

One of the principal areas in which the Lord is anxious to heal us is the nagging distress and worry caused when we doubt his forgiveness of our past sins. This interior disturbance is not from God; he is a God of peace and the very source of our peace. The turmoil we experience could well be one of the insidious wiles of the devil to get us discouraged. When we meet the Lord regularly in the Sacrament of Reconciliation, he always touches us with his healing love. Gradually our doubts and fears about our former sins will be healed and we will experience that peace of mind and heart which only the Lord can give.

EUCHARISTIC CELEBRATION

The Sacrifice of the Mass is the second powerful means that the Lord instituted to convey his forgiveness and healing. The eucharistic celebration is both a sacrament and a sacrifice through which Jesus channels his forgiveness and healing to us. The Mass is the most sublime act of worship we can offer. Uniting ourselves with Jesus in the eucharistic celebration conveys not only his mercy and compassion to us, but also strengthens our confidence, which is an effective antidote to overcome any misgivings we may have about the forgiveness of those pesky past sins. Our offering the Mass will also enkindle within us a genuine spirit of gratitude and appreciation of his unbounded forgiving love.

The prayers of the Mass will create a contrite, humble heart within us, thus helping us to form a proper disposition to receive forgiveness and healing. We begin the Mass with the Penitential Rite in which we pause to acknowledge silently our sinfulness, to repent and beg the Lord's forgiveness. If we offer the Mass regularly, even daily, it would be more fruitful to single out a particular fault for which we need forgiveness and healing rather than recalling our sinfulness in general. Gradually, as we overcome one or other failing, we are forming the mind and heart of Jesus within us.

LITURGY OF THE WORD

In the Liturgy of the Word, how often the readings remind us of the Lord's mercy and compassion. In the first and second reading we learn of the Lord's eagerness to forgive. In the Old

Testament, speaking to us through the prophet Isaiah, our heavenly Father assures us that his love will never leave us nor will his covenant of mercy ever change (Is 54:10). This is only one of the many times the writers of the Old Testament confirm God's willingness to forgive. To mention only one of the New Testament's many references to the Lord's forgiveness, Paul writes, "Where sin increased, grace overflowed all the more" (Rom 5:20). The responsorial psalm frequently confirms the Lord's desire to forgive and the actual implementation of his desire. Listen to only one of the many occasions when the psalmist assures us: "He pardons all your iniquities, he heals all your ills" (Ps 103:3).

The Gospel, too, records the many teachings of Jesus on his forgiving love, and the many occasions when Jesus forgave anyone who came to him with faith and sorrow. How often Jesus says, "Your sins are forgiven."

LITURGY OF THE EUCHARIST

The words of Jesus speak to us eloquently about why he instituted this redemptive sacrifice. Repeating the words of Jesus at the Consecration of the Mass the celebrant says, "Take this, all of you, and eat it: this is my body which will be given for you." Likewise, the words spoken in consecrating the wine leave no doubt about the Lord's willingness to forgive, "Take this, all of you, and drink from it; this is the cup of my blood, the blood of the new and everlasting covenant. It will be shed for you and for all so that sins may be forgiven" (Sacramentary, page 519). If there is still some concern in your heart about being included in the forgiveness of our sins, notice the Lord's invitation: "Take this, *all* of you..." and again: "It will be shed for you and for *all*...." We need to remember that this is God's solemn promise. Dare we have any further doubts?

COMMUNION RITE

We begin the Communion Rite with the Lord's Prayer in which we beg, "Forgive us our trespasses as we forgive those who trespass against us." Perhaps we may wonder if we have really forgiven those who have offended us. We must remind ourselves that if we could totally and completely forgive others, it would be a special gift from the Lord and not of our own doing. All that he asks of us is that we are striving to the best of our ability to forgive others. Perhaps a better rendition would read, "Forgive us our trespasses as we are striving to forgive those who trespass against us." Forgiveness is an act of our will regardless of how we feel about it.

Immediately following the Lord's Prayer in the Communion Rite, we pray for peace and also for protection from all anxiety. We would do well to pray this prayer frequently and fervently to free us of all anxiety about our past sins.

Deliver us, Lord, from every evil,
    and grant us peace in our day.
In your mercy keep us free from sin
    and protect us from all anxiety
As we wait in joyful hope
    for the coming of our Savior, Jesus Christ.

As we come to the immediate preparation for receiving Holy Communion, we admit once more our unworthiness and assure ourselves of his forgiveness and healing. "Lord, I am not worthy to receive you, but only say the word and I shall be healed." These words should remove from our hearts any doubt or fear of not being forgiven.

Prayer for the Forgiveness of Sin:

Lord, hear the prayers of those who call on you, forgive the sins of those who confess to you, and in your merciful love, give us pardon and peace. Amen

EPILOGUE

I offer these pages with the hope that the example and fortitude of those people enduring a painful loss may bring inspiration and comfort, hope and encouragement to anyone with a similar tragedy. Most of the people I encountered were able to endure their loss when they were convinced in their own heart that God loves them with a caring, concerned love, and that he permits certain suffering and pain, disappointment and loss to condition us in this land of exile for the unimaginable peace and happiness awaiting us in the world to come. They also found that suffering helped them to keep their focus on the Lord.

In their affliction they listened and responded to the Lord's invitation, "Come to me, all you who labor and are burdened, and I will give you rest" (Mt 11:28). Throughout the pages of this book, we have been reminded that the Lord is our constant companion, our comforter and our healer who will never permit anything to happen to us from which he cannot bring some good. He is always eager to touch us with his healing love and power when we approach him with an expectant faith and an unwavering trust.

When the two blind men begged Jesus to heal them, he asked an important question, "Do you believe that I can do this?" (Mt 9:28). When they assured him that they did believe, he cured them of their blindness. The Lord poses the same question to us. When we turn to him seeking his help with faith and confidence, with humility and trust, we can be certain that he will respond in some way to our need. He may not heal us physically nor instantly, but he will heal us inside by giving us the insight and strength, the serenity and peace of mind and heart to accept our affliction with calm and courage.

NOTES

ONE
Why, Lord?

1. Pope John XXIII, *Journal of a Soul*, translated from the Italian by Dorothy White (New York, N.Y.: McGraw-Hill, 1965).

THREE
At Peace with Ourselves

1. From the Communion Rite of Mass.

SEVEN
Daily Burdens

1. From the score "Naughty Marietta," *Family Song Book* (Pleasantville, N.Y.: Reader's Digest Assoc., 1969), 164.

TEN
Crisis of Alcohol Addiction

1. Anthony de Mello, *Hearts of Fire* (St. Louis, Mo.: Institute of Jesuit Studies, 1993), 75.

FIFTEEN
Death and Dying

1. From the Sacramentary, 931.